ea | *reproduced by kind permission of Lord St Oswald.*

In the Shadow of a Saint

Lady Alice More

In the Shadow of a Saint

Lady Alice More

RUTH NORRINGTON

For
Thomas

Designed by Peter Tucker, typeset in Bembo
and printed at The Alden Press, Oxford

The Kylin Press, Darbonne House, Waddesdon, Buckinghamshire
© Ruth Norrington, 1983
ISBN 0 907128 13 0

Contents

List of Illustrations

Foreword

G REAT MEN'S WOMEN often get bad press, whether deserved or not. Dame Alice More's hitherto bad press has been undeserved, as this absorbing book convincingly shows. With her mother-wit, long nose, strong character and practical gifts, she rightly became More's diminutive '*lion*'. By one of the ironies of history, the direct descendants of Alice are better known than those of Thomas. Through her first marriage to John Middleton she was to become the ancestress of Lady Hester Stanhope, the eccentric Eastern traveller; Lord Cholmondeley, the Lord Great Chamberlain, takes his family title of Rock Savage from her great great grandson; and most surprising of all — the Royal Family are themselves direct descendants through the Earls of Strathmore. Dame Alice was also a kinswoman of Henry VIII.

A full life of Dame Alice More has long been needed, and Ruth Norrington fills the gap with charm, humanity and dedicated diligence. She has unearthed facts that have laid hidden for over four centuries. Her narrative emerges with a new all-round picture of the Mores' life in the city and in Chelsea that can only be described as a 'merry' one. The word '*merry*', which occurs so often in the Tudor texts quoted by Lady Norrington, has been sadly relegated today to the Christmas card!

Best of all, Ruth Norrington does credit to Sir Thomas More's own judgment, by showing that the Saint, far from choosing a mere stepmother-housekeeper for his children and wards, and an additional hair-shirt for himself, selected a woman capable of building with him a rare family community, in which laughter and jokes were the framework for prayer.

Elizabeth Longford

Prologue

'Tilly vally, Tilly vally, Master More,
what-the-good-year?'

AS I SIT IN THE SHADE of the old brick wall of my aunt's garden in Chelsea, one of the few boundary walls of More's Chelsea estate still standing, the sharp tone of the voice, tinged with love and humour, seems to drift over it. The chatter and laughter of the family group sitting round the ancient mulberry tree on the other side ring down four hundred and fifty years. The owner of the Great House, one of England's greatest and most loved saints, is trying the patience of his wife beyond endurance.

'Tilly vally, Tilly vally, Master More,
what-the-good-year?'

Walking along the passage that leads from the hall of the Governor's house in the Tower of London, down a few steps into the octagonal chamber, where More spent the last fifteen months of his life, I seem to hear the ghostly voice again. This time the bantering good humour is changed to fearful urgency as Dame Alice, in her despair, begs this most obstinate of men to save his own life.

'What the good year? I marvel that you,
that have always hitherto been taken for so wise a man,
will now so play the fool as to lie here in this filthy prison.'

What does shine through all More's mention of his wife is that he was deeply devoted to her, and enjoyed her company enormously. He loved a joke, and had a great sense of humour. Lady Alice was not only a good foil for his teasing ways, but she also gave him as good as she got in wit and repartee, as well as twenty four years of loving devotion to himself and his children.

A detail from the Holbein painting of the More family, now at Nostell Priory / reproduced by kind permission of Lord St Oswald.

Dame Alice was lovable, down to earth, born to tease and be teased. This pillar of respectability, rich widow of a London silk merchant, John Middleton, arrives on the scene in More's biographies with dramatic abruptness. Barely three weeks after the death of his first wife, Jane Colt, probably in childbed, in 1511, More makes an unexpected visit to his parish priest, Father Bouge, a Carthusian, late on a Sunday night. Father Bouge was vicar of St Stephen's, Walbrook, and a friend and fellow student of John Fisher, Bishop of St Stephen's, The priest is astonished at the visit and the lateness of the hour. Let him take up the story in his own words in a letter written to Dame Catherine Manne in 1535, after More's execution:

> 'He was my parishioner in London. I christened him two godley children. I buried his first wife. And within a month after, he came to me on a Sunday late at night, and there he brought me a dispensation from Cuthbert Tunstall, to be married the next day with no banns asking'[1]

Tunstall was then Chancellor to Archibishop Warham, and later became Bishop of London, and in 1530, Bishop of Durham.

There is no mention of Mistress Alice in any of More's correspondence prior to this night's interview with the priest, but within a week she was his wife, mistress of his household and stepmother to his four young children. Margaret, the eldest, was aged six, Elizabeth was five, Cecily four, and John, the baby, two. The death toll in Tudor times, especially in childbirth, was heavy, and remarriage, especially where young children were involved, more or less a foregone conclusion. But even for those times, More's very hasty marriage so soon after the death of his first wife was looked upon as unusual, and even, by some of his friends, as unwise. More and his first wife, Jane, both had large families who could have helped him with the children after her death.

Mistress Alice Middleton, widow, when she walked up the aisle of St Stephen's Church, Walbrook, in the City of London, in the autumn of 1511, to marry Master Thomas More, must have wondered about her future. Her bridegroom was a widower, a man she had known some years. She had also known his first wife who lay in her three-week-old grave in the churchyard only a few yards from her. But if she had been told that her second husband was to become one of England's most famous and popular saints, she would have received the news with total incredulity, expressions such as *'Tilly vally, what-the-good-year'*, and a great deal of laughter. Saints are not born but made, and in the untidy, clever, teasing and intolerant man she saw beside her, she may have already seen the signs of a tendency to religious fanaticism, but of sanctity, definitely not.

But that she did play a significant, colourful and memorable part in the growth and sanctification of her husband cannot be doubted; not, as is so popularly imagined, by being an extra irritation to the hair shirt that he always wore, and of which she so violently disapproved, but as his constant companion, friend, overseer of his large household, devoted stepmother to his four young children, and not least the much loved wife who always made him laugh, even in the last terrible days in the Tower.

Father Bridgett, in his biography, writes that it was More's fate in his lifetime, as it has been since, to have his jokes taken seriously. Dame Alice's reputation has suffered because of this. The bantering teasing tones of her husband were a sign of deep affection, and her sharp retorts, often giving as good as she got in repartee, were More's delight. Posterity still tends to see her as the plain, *'beak-nosed harpie'* of Ammonio's description, or *'nec bella ad modum neu puella'* (neither a pearl nor a girl) which Erasmus grudgingly admitted was only a family joke.

Perhaps one of the most damaging of these *'devil's advocates'*, if I may use such a phrase of such a man, is More himself. Some people think that he carried the jokes against his wife too far in his life time, although I am sure she was a match for them. What I feel he did not envisage was that his jokes about her, after their deaths, would have crystallized into an exaggerated picture of a woman who does not truly resemble the wife he was devoted to. I hope in the following pages to do what I am sure he would have wanted someone to do, to attempt at least to put the picture of her a little more in perspective. It is of vital importance to a person's good reputation that a biographer should have a liking and sympathy for his or her subject. Most people would rather be written about after their death by their children than their stepchildren, by a real great grandson, rather than a step-great grandson, and by a friend of their own rather than a very critical friend of their husband's. The less favourable alternatives have so far been Dame Alice's fate and it is important to assess the relationship between these early writers and herself if we are to do her justice.

Erasmus, More's great friend, wrote a brief description of the family after the publication of *Utopia* in 1518. The early relationship between Dame Alice and this brilliant but pernickety scholar, as I will mention in more detail, left much to be desired, although after knowing her for twenty-three years he did become an admirer, albeit rather grudgingly.

William Roper, her stepson-in-law, husband of More's eldest daughter

Margaret, is our next source. He was definitely not the man to do her justice. Writing his short *Life of More* as a guide to the larger biography he had asked Nicholas Harpsfield to write at least twenty years after More's death, he shows little sympathy for her, and was in fact, a man who, although lost in admiration for his saintly father-in-law, never really understood him either. His insensitivity even led him to endeavour to deprive Dame Alice, after More's death, of part of her income, in spite of his own considerable wealth. Dame Alice had little good to expect from him.

Harpsfield, a scholar of Winchester and New College, Oxford, having fled to Louvain in 1550, to be near some of the More family, the Clements and Rastells, who were also exiled there, had the same version of Dame Alice from Roper. Cresacre More, More's great grandson, also got his information from stories handed down from Dame Alice's stepchildren and, therefore, the bias against her is still there. Stapleton, writing in 1588, gives a more accurate picture of Alice, omitting the unkind characterisation of the earlier works, and having as his sources family letters not used by Roper and Harpsfield, provided by Dorothy Colly. More's later biographer, Professor Raymond Wilson Chambers himself wrote in 1926, to Mrs Mary Probert *'it looks as if Mistress Alice Middleton has been an old family friend. Everything seems to point to a group of families closely connected and inter-married.'* Chambers and E. E. Reynolds begin to see her in correct perspective. Father Bridgett protests against the attempts to blacken the character of the good lady, he writes:

> *'We have now heard all the evil that can be alleged against this lady, and it certainly does not justify our classing Blessed Thomas More amongst the ill-matched great men. To say that when his time of suffering came she did not rise to the height of his soul, is merely to class her with nearly all of her contemporaries, including almost every abbess, abbot and bishop in the country'.*[2]

Theodore Maynard refers to her as *'the tart-tongued and salty Dame Alice who was so racy a character that her husband greatly relished her exquisite blend of common sense and absurdity.'* Father Bernard Basset, in his book says:

> *'A great many unkind things have been said about her, few of them justified. More was devoted to her, and much in her debt. Only a woman of her uninhibited tastes could have faced such a situation, and played such a notable part in building up one of the most distinguished households in Europe'.*[3]

Professor Chambers tells us that in the nineteen thirties a young member of the Alington family, when told by his mother that he was not descended from Sir Thomas More, but from his wife, Dame Alice, sighed with relief, and replied, *'Thank goodness for that. She was the only one of the whole lot who had any sense'*. Dame Alice and her husband would have been highly amused at such a remark in a young descendant of hers.

The Tomb of Sir Peter Ardern with Brasses of him and his wife Katherine Bohun
in Latton church, Essex /
reproduced by kind permission of the Bodleian Library, Oxford.

An Ardern Mystery

*'Her nose was a nose of wild ambitions, of pride grown fantastical,
a nose that scorned the earth shooting off, one fancies,
towards some eternally eccentric heaven. It was a nose,
in fact, altogether in the air. Noses, of course, are aristocratic things,
and Lady Hester was the child of a great aristocracy.'*

LYTTON STRACHEY was describing a prominent feature of Lady Hester Stanhope. She was the eldest daughter of Charles, 3rd Earl Stanhope, Jacobin and inventor, who made the first steam-boat, the first calculating machine, who defended the French Revolution in the House of Lords, and erased the armorial bearings – *'Damned aristocratic nonsense'* – from his carriages and plate. These two remarkable people, father and daughter, were directly descended from Lady Alice More.

Strangely enough one of the few facts that have been known about Alice was the size of her nose. She was unkindly dubbed *'a beak-nosed harpy'* by Ammonio, Henry VIII's Latin Secretary. We know, from Holbein's drawing of her for the family portrait, that the description was grossly exaggerated. Lady Alice was married to More and ruled over his household for twenty-four years, and she probably knew him better than any one else. Why do we know so little about her?

In searching for her identity before she married her first husband, John Middleton, it almost appeared as if her descendant, the 3rd Earl Stanhope, having finished the job of erasing his own armorial bearings from his carriages and plate, had been at work erasing all traces that otherwise might have been available to the researchers into the origin of his ancestress, Lady More. Or she may, herself, when the troubled times came immediately before More's execution, and during the long years after it, have deliberately destroyed any available documents and other means of identification, whose presence might have involved her and her daughter and grandchildren in More's disgrace.

Whatever the reasons may be, she has remained an elusive figure, and the search for her ascendants and descendants has been difficult but fascinating, and in some instances very rewarding.

Looking in on my television at the 1979 opening of Parliament by Her Majesty the Queen, with all its pomp and splendour, I realised that four of the main participants in the stately procession that wound its way to the Chamber of the House of Lords for the Speech from the Throne, made a family party of Lady Alice's descendants! Firstly Lord Chomondeley, the Lord Great Chamberlain, slowly walking backwards at the head of the procession, who takes one of his titles, used by his eldest son, Earl Rocksavage, from Lady Alice's great grandson, the first Viscount Savage of Rocksavage. The Richmond Herald, Michael Maclagan, dressed in his colourful tabard, himself a direct descendant of Lady Alice. Facing the Lord Great Chamberlain, with the Imperial State Crown glittering on her head in the dazzling lights, came Her Majesty, Queen Elizabeth the Second, granddaughter of Lady Alice eleven generations removed through direct descent, with her son, the Prince of Wales.

On 1 July 1960, at the Globe Theatre, London, Robert Bolt's masterly play, *A Man For All Seasons* was given its first performance. In his description of the cast, Mr. Bolt's comment on Dame Alice is wonderfully apt: *'Absurd at a distance, impressive close to'*. With keen perception, as his play progresses, he penetrates deeply into the heart of More and his dilemma, and in doing so, has drawn us closer to his wife than any previous writer has done.

Sir Richard Harpur was the father of Alice, thus Bolt got nearer the truth as to her identity than he could have imagined. The Harpur arms are a lion rampant. In the moving farewell scene between More and his wife, he pays her a great tribute:-

'Why, it's a lion I married, a lion, a lion!'

The mystery of Dame Alice's parentage has remained unsolved for four hundred years, and there are only a few facts on which to base a search for her identity. However, two vital clues have been spared from the ravages of time, the devastation of the bombs of war, and the demolition of the bulldozer of peace.

The first clue, known to most lovers of More, is the epitaph in Chelsea Old Church. The building had a direct hit in an air raid in April, 1941, and was demolished, all save the More Chapel and the Holbein capitals. The epitaph, written by More for himself and his two wives, was shattered, but was skilfully put together again. What is seen today, following its restoration after the war, shows the arms of the Colt family for his first wife, and the arms of the Warwickshire Arderns for his second. The heraldry over it, of which I will say more later, at least tells us that More's second wife was entitled to bear the arms of the Ardern family, but whether through her father, mother, or grandfather, was not known.

The second clue is found in the beautiful countryside of Essex, not far from Netherhall where More's first wife, Jane Colt was born. Here another kind of devastation took place after the war, this time the bulldozers moved in. From the destruction of several quiet hamlets and thousands of acres of farmland, Harlow New Town was created, the first development of its kind in the country. Near the centre in an oasis of green, formed by the remants of the great park of Markhall, still stands the Church of St Mary-at-Latton. To the north of the chancel is its greatest glory, the little chantry chapel of Sir Peter Ardern, who died in 1467, built for himself and his wife, Katherine Bohun, in 1447. His tomb and that of his wife lie in the chancel and beside it is that of his son-in-law, Sir Richard Harpur, who died in 1492. The latter's wife, Elizabeth Ardern, is depicted in brass beside him. She was the younger daughter of Sir Peter, and his co-heiress with her sister Anne, for Sir Peter had no male heirs. Underneath Sir Richard and his wife, were brasses of their three sons and one daughter. The brass of the sons is still there, but only the indent of the daughter survives, the brass is missing. It is thanks to the observant eye of Richard Gough two hundred years ago when the brass was still intact, that we know that it depicted a young lady, dressed like her mother, *'kith after kind'* in the height of fashion, the future wife of St Thomas More.

Alice herself mentions her mother as a woman of strong character, *'not wishing to be ruled, but to rule',* and More's great grandson, Cresacre More, mentions that Alice's mother was a very talkative woman, like her daughter, *'kith after kind'.*

Alice's first husband, John Middleton, who died in 1509, mentions in his will that his wife brought some fortune into their marriage, presumably from the Ardern family.

The most logical approach to the problem of Alice's parentage seems to be to trace the Ardern families who were entitled to bear the arms now displayed on the epitaph, the most senior of these being the Warwickshire Arderns of Parkhall. Their lineage is ancient, going back before the Conquest to Saxon times and these arms, *'ermine a fesse checky or and azure'* are some of the oldest in heraldry.

Walter Ardern of Parkhall, whose father Robert Ardern was executed in 1452 for taking the Yorkist side in the Wars of the Roses, married Eleanor Hampden, daughter of John Hampden of Buckinghamshire. He had ten children, six sons and four daughters, the youngest of whom was called Alice, born about 1470.[4] This Alice Ardern of Parkhall married a man called Buckland, and a mention of her in the will of her brother, John Ardern, in 1526,[5] as still bearing that name must exclude her from the possibility that she might have been More's wife. Professor Chambers mentions Alice's likeness in a speech to Shakespeare's Mistress Quickly.[6] As Shakespeare's mother was descended from the Ardens of Parkhall, it was a charming thought that the Lady Alice might have been the poet's great great aunt.

The second branch of the Arderns who were entitled to the same coat of Arms were the Arderns of Cottisford, a junior branch of the Warwickshire Arderns. Here in the heart of Oxfordshire, in one of the villages made famous by Flora Thompson in *Lark rise to Candleford,* still stands the ancient old manor house where the Arderns lived for about one hundred and fifty years, from 1460 to 1606, with a magnificent timbered roof and a view of the old parish church opposite, where many Arderns were buried. The hunt for Alice has certainly drawn nearer London which was her home after her marriage to John Middleton. The land adjacent to the manor of Cottisford is the manor of Fringford which was acquired by More in 1525. Cottisford belonged to Eton College in the late fifteenth century, and here a daughter was born to William Ardern, their tenant, in about 1470.[7] But she, in fact, married Thomas Thorne of Northamptonshire, and there is no reason to suppose that he died soon enough for her to marry John Middleton, as her second husband, in the late 1490's, and then Thomas More in 1511. In her brother John's will, which is in the Oxford Diocesan Records, he makes no mention of his sister, yet we know that Lady Alice was very much alive in 1535 when this will was made. There were Arderns in Beverley and Marton in Yorkshire, but I could find no trace of any Alice Ardern later than 1405, and their arms were not the same. However, it will be revealed later how they were to play an important part in identifying Lady Alice's family.

The great speed with which More remarried after the death of his first wife strongly suggested that the lady of his choice was a great friend of his family, and someone who knew his late wife, Jane Colt, well. One theory has been put forward that the wife of Jane's brother, Thomas Colt, Magdalen Middleton, was Alice's eldest daughter.[8] If Alice Middleton had a daughter called Magdalen who married Thomas Colt, More and Alice might well have met in Jane's lifetime through this connection. But there is no evidence for the connection, and conclusive evidence against it. When John Middleton made his Will and died in

1509 he had two unmarried daughters, Alice and Helen, and left dowries for them on their marriage, his estate to his wife Alice for her life, and after her death to be divided equally between his two daughters, or the whole estate to a surviving daughter, if one of these should die before their mother.[9] The omission of the name of a third daughter would only be possible if by then she was already married (or dead). But the date rules out marriage to Thomas Colt. Jane's eldest brother George lived until 1578 and was probably born, therefore, after 1500, certainly not more than two or three years earlier. Thomas was the second son, and well under marriageable age in 1509.[10] John Colt, his father, left a bequest in his will, in 1522, to Sir Thomas More, of ten marks yearly, for the *'finding'* of his son Thomas until he came of age. This means that the Mores probably took the young Thomas into their household until he was twenty-one, and proves that he could not have been born earlier than 1502, which would make him not more than seven years old at the time of John Middleton's death.[11]

A reference to property, near Chelmsford,[12] still held by Lady Alice after More's death, switched the search for her origins down to the area in Essex where the Colt family had their estate, and where Jane spent the first sixteen years of her life, until her marriage to More in 1505. Their property was Netherhall, a mile and a half south west of Royden. A gatehouse and curtain wall

A rare engraving of the early Tudor house of Netherhall / The Kylin Archive.

The church of St Mary's-at-Latton / Mrs Ewen Dymond.

of an early Tudor house, built of brick, with blue brick diaper, still remains. One of the two towers on either side of the gateway is still standing, three stories high. Owing to the collapse of the other, it is possible to look into the guardroom beyond, and a number of rooms beside it. During a recent visit there was a charming notice pinned to the gate reminding one of the Colt family and their arms, *'argent a fesse azure between three colts full speed sable'.* The notice read, *Please shut the gate. Pony loose!*

In the nearby church of St Peter's, Royden, are the tombs of the Colt family, partly obscured by the altar of the Colt Chapel. Thomas Colt, a Chancellor of the Exchequer to Edward IV, lies on one side of it and on the other John Colt, father of Jane, and his wife Jane Elrington, who was the aunt as it happened of Alice's first son-in-law to be, (by her first marriage to John Middleton) Thomas Elrington.[13]

The nearby estate of Markhall, now engulfed by Harlow New Town, still has its church of St Mary-at-Latton, beautifully preserved on a green hillock, surrounded by trees from the old estate. The drive to the manor still winds up to the north side of the church, but the old manor house has long been demolished, and the church hall has been built on its site. Entering through a low Tudor door on the north side of the church, one finds the original Chantry Chapel of the Arden family, still intact, with its wall paintings just visible and a grill and squint in its south wall, giving a view of the main altar of the church, and the tomb of Sir Peter Ardern, Chief Baron of the Exchequer, Justice of the King's Bench, and Serjeant-at-law, and his wife Katherine.

Sir Peter was Deputy Steward of the Duchy of Lancaster in 1440, under William de la Pole. He took the Order of the Coif in 1443, became a Serjeant-at-Law. He bought the Markhall estate in 1446, became Baron of the Exchequer in 1461, and Justice of the King's bench in 1467, just before his death. He built the Chantry Chapel in 1447, as a burial place for himself and his wife and for masses to be said in perpetuity for their souls and the souls of his family.[14] He married Katherine Bohun, a member of the great Bohun family, who had been Earls of Hereford, Northampton, and Essex, and Constables of England. Sir Peter had no sons, and the great wealth he had accumulated in land, jewellery, plate and books was left to his wife and two daughters, Anne and Elizabeth.[15] At the time of his death, his daughter Anne was married to a kinsman of her mother's, Sir John Bohun, son and heir of Humphrey Bohun. His family came from Midhurst, Sussex, and he had inherited the manor of Filiol's (Felix Hall), Kellvedon in Essex, and the adjoining estate of Feering and Great Baxted.[16] Anne and John Bohun only had two daughters, Mary and Ursula. Mary married Sir David Owen, natural son of Owen Tudor, grandfather of Henry VII, and thus, the Ardern family became kinsmen of Henry VIII.[17] Ursula, the younger sister, married Robert Southwell, who was a great friend of Henry. VII [18]

Sir Peter Ardern left both his estates of Markhall and Enfield, (which he held from the Duchy of Lancaster), to his wife for her life, and on her death Markhall went to Anne Bohun, and Enfield to his younger daughter Elizabeth. She was a woman of forceful character, who married three times, and outlived all her husbands, inheriting their property and acting as their executor. Her first husband, to whom she was married at the time of Sir Peter's death, was Sir John Skreene, a minor, and ward of her father. There were no children of this marriage. He was trained as a lawyer, and was descended from William Skreene, Serjeant-at-Law to Henry IV. His property included Stanford Rivers, Chambers, Writtle and Roxwell, near Chelmsford, in Essex. He died in 1474 leaving his estates for life to Elizabeth, and a collection of splendid legal books which had been left to him by his father-in-law.[19] He was only twenty four.

Soon after his death Elizabeth embarked on her second marriage, this time to Sir Richard Harpur, of Epping. He purchased the manor of Latton, adjacent to

Markhall, in 1485, and they appear to have lived there until his death in 1492.[20]

It is from the brasses on his tomb, that lies on the floor, beside that of Sir Peter Ardern and his wife, in the chancel of St Mary-at-Latton, that the clue as to the identity of Dame Alice came. It is an armorial clue, and we shall need the aid of heraldry to follow it up.

Harpur lies there in armour with a whippet at his feet, and a sword across his body, with his wife beside him, slightly turned towards him. She is dressed in the

The Tomb of Sir Richard Harpur: brasses of Sir Richard, his wife, three sons and one daughter, from Gough's Maps, 1798 / reproduced by kind permission of the Bodleian Library, Oxford.

height of fashion, with an elaborate ornament round her neck. Above his head are the arms of the Harpur family and above Elizabeth's head are the arms of the Arderns impaled with the Harpur arms.

When Richard Gough described the brass in 1798, the shield below the figure of Sir Richard was missing, as well as the inscription, but the shield below his wife was the Ardern arms on their own. Since Gough saw this tomb the Ardern arms have been moved across, from Elizabeth, and are now beneath her husband. But what Gough did see below Elizabeth was a brass of her daughter, a young woman dressed in the height of fashion, like her mother. This effigy is now, alas, missing. But the existence of one daughter of Elizabeth Ardern's marriage to Richard Harpur is beyond doubt. Her adult costume indicates that she would have been about seventeen years old at the time of her father's death, and therefore the eldest child. As there is no mention of her in her father's will, she was already married and provided for.[21]

Sir Peter Ardern's daughters were not only heiresses to his estates, they were also his heraldic heiresses; that is, in the absence of any male heirs to their father, they were entitled to bear his arms themselves and pass on this right to all their children, whether male or female. Thus the daughter of Elizabeth Ardern, would, on the death of her mother, have the right to display the Ardern arms, hence their presence on the More epitaph in Chelsea.

This one daughter of Elizabeth Ardern's from her marriage to Sir Richard Harpur was Alice, the Alice we are looking for, who was first married as a young girl to John Middleton, and secondly, two years after his death to Thomas More. This means that she was an heiress of Sir Peter Ardern of Markhall, not of William Ardern of Parkhall, Warwickshire.

The age given for Alice, granddaughter of Sir Peter Ardern, on the Holbein sketch of the family, now in the Basle Museum, must be inaccurate. As the eldest child of Sir Richard Harpur she was born about 1475, and therefore at the time of the drawing was fifty-four years old not fifty-seven. The sketch was drawn some time between the years 1527 and 1529, and acknowledged by Erasmus to whom it was sent, in 1529. The ages on the drawing are not written in More's hand, and may have been jotted in beside the figures by Nicholas Kratzer, the mathmetician, astronomer and wit, who several years before had been, for a short time, tutor in the More household.[22] The ages of the children are correct, as might have been expected, but the age of More has never been firmly established, some authorities giving his birth as 1477 and others as 1478. Kratzer, if it was he, may have mistaken Alice's age. It is, of course, definitely known that she was older than More.

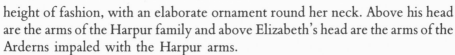

A more difficult problem is the fact that the Ardern arms displayed on the tombs in the church of St Mary-at-Latton are not the same as those on the existing More epitaph in Chelsea Old Church. How is it that the wrong arms are displayed on the Chelsea Epitaph? The answer lies in the very checkered history of the epitaph itself.

John Weever, in his *Funeral Monuments,*[23] *Richard Newcourt, in his Repertorium,*[24] Stowe's *Survey of London,*[25] and John Aubrey, in his *Brief Lives,*[26] all agree that the original epitaph designed by More was a very simple affair, not the display of heraldry that we see today. Aubrey writes:

> *'The tomb was near the middle of the south wall (of the church),
> where some slight monument was erected, which being worn by time, about
> 1644, Sir John Lawrence at his own proper cost and charge, erected to his
> memory a handsome, faire inscription of marble.'*

They all also agree that by the seventeenth century the stone was so worn as to be nearly indecipherable. At the time that More had this epitaph erected in the church, he had already fallen from the Royal favour, and was beginning to worry about any repercussions that might ultimately fall on his wife and family. In this situation it seems more likely that he would have designed a simple monument for his message to posterity about himself, with his own arms above it, but not one that made a great display of the families of his two wives.

In 1644 Sir John Lawrence redesigned the epitaph and refurbished it in a manner he thought fitting for the great Lord Chancellor and his family, and it is this design that we see more or less today. It could have been at this time, when the words of he epitaph were cut in black marble, that the heraldic devices of his two wives were placed above it with his own, and separately. That Lady Alice had been an Ardern heiress was remembered, but the mistake of placing the arms of the older branch of the family, instead of the younger, is one that is easily understood. They may even have been put there deliberately by Sir John to add even greater dignity to the monument. Those wishing to decry More had often mentioned his humble origins, with no great ancestry behind him, and to impale one of the oldest arms in heraldry with his would have appealed to the designer.

There is a second consideration which should not be discounted, and that is the similarity between the names of the two estates of the Ardern families, the older branch coming from Parkhall, and the younger from Markhall. Sir John was redesigning the tomb nearly a hundred years after Lady More's death, and some confusion of names and arms would have been understandable.

In 1832 the gallery that had partly obscured the epitaph was removed, and it again appeared to be in a very dilapidated state. This time it was restored by John Faulkner, a stone mason of Chelsea, and was described by Thomas Faulkner in glowing terms:

'It imitated and preserved the antique style of the various mouldings, frieze and foliage, so that the whole monument now displays a uniform appearance, equally creditable to the artist, and those who performed the work.'

This indicated that further alterations were made, providing another chance for the armorial blazonings to go awry.

Mr John Faulkner was apparently faced with the criticism that his restoration was not true to the original. He fiercely defended his work in an article in the Gentleman's Magazine in 1833.[27] He refers to a *'slight drawing'* in the Harleian MSS of the tomb in about 1620, looking similar to his own restoration. The manuscript is mentioned again in Beaver's *Memorials of old Chelsea,*[28] but in both these cases without a reference number. It occurs again in Randall Davies' *Chelsea Old Church,*[29] and Stowe's *Survey of London,* the reference being given as Vol 2113, Fol 114b. This folio number does not now exist as it was altered to folio number 175b in 1880. The drawing is, in fact, of an elaborate version of the More arms which were on the walls of Chelsea Old Church, showing five quarterings. Quarters one and two are the arms of More's father showing the moorcocks, three is *ermine a fesse checky or and azure* for the Ardern family, four is *gules three coronets a bordure engrailed,* and five *or a cross gules voided of the field.* So much for Mr Faulkner's slight drawing. A careful search by the writer and by the staff of the MSS department of the British Library reveals the arms quoted above, but nothing more. This linking of his wife's arms in a quartering with his own is against heraldic usage, as More and Alice had no children, which is a strong argument for an ill-informed heraldic designer.

Mr Moore of Boston, writing in 1889, mentions this odd coat of arms which was on the wall of Chelsea old Church, and remarks on the mystery of no maiden name being given for Lady Alice.[30] The armorial tinctures were again repainted in 1935, and this time poor Alice's arms appear as *'ermine a fesse gules'.*[31] Finally in 1941 the whole monument was shattered by a bomb, and had to be restored once more.

The correct arms of Lady Alice, those of the Arderns of Essex, not of Warwickshire, should be placed on the epitaph at Chelsea, putting her, at last, in her rightful place, as granddaughter, and heiress of Sir Peter Ardern of Markhall, close neighbour of the Colt family of Netherhall.

*The church of St Katherine's Coleman, where John Middleton was buried /
by kind permission of the Rev. L.E.M. Claxton.*

Mistress Alice Middleton

'a very eligible widow'

For the last forty years of her life, Alice was known to the world as Mistress More, Lady More, Lady Alice More, or sometimes, Dame Alice. For about fifteen years previous to that she was known as Mistress Alice Middleton. For the first sixteen years of her life, as the only daughter of Sir Richard Harpur and Elizabeth Ardern, and granddaughter of Sir Peter Ardern, she was Miss Alice Harpur.

As a member of the Ardern family, of Markhall, Essex, and near neighbour of the Colt family of Netherhall, the reasons for More wanting to marry her so soon after the death of his first wife, Jane Colt, become clearer. Further research into the Ardern and Colt families, and More's connection with them, shows that More probably knew his second wife before he knew his first.

Thomas Colt, Jane's grandfather, was Chancellor of the Exchequer to Edward IV, and Sir Peter Ardern, who bought the estate near him in Essex, as a Baron of the Exchequer, was a colleague of his. More's father, as a budding young lawyer, knew them both, and followed in Sir Peter Ardern's footsteps as Sergent-at-Law and Justice of the King's Bench. John More's property of Gobions, at North Mimms, Hertfordshire, was about twenty-five miles from the Colt and Ardern estates.

Sir Richard Harpur bought the manor of Latton, adjacent to Markhall, in 1485, when his daughter was about ten years old. He died in 1492, leaving Latton and another estate nearby called Chambers, to his wife Elizabeth.[32] His daughter was then seventeen, and their neighbour, Jane Colt, three years old. Harpur made Sir Reginald Bray executor of his estate, and left him a silver cup in his will. The Bray family were to have a long and close connection with Alice and her grandchildren.

The date of Alice's marriage to John Middleton is unknown, but she is mentioned as his wife in a deed in connection with some property in Uxbridge in 1499. As she is not mentioned in her father's will, she was already married and provided for at the time of his death in 1492.[33]

Elizabeth Ardern's third husband was Sir Andrew Dymoke. He is mentioned with Sir Richard Harpur in entries in the *Calendar of Patent Rolls* in 1486 and 1489, prior to Sir Richard's death. He was therefore well acquainted with the family and also became a Baron of the Exchequer in 1500.

In 1501 Elizabeth's brother-in-law, husband of her sister Anne, Sir John Bohun, died, and Anne sold the Markhall estate to Sir John Shaa. He was Lord Mayor of London, a prominent goldsmith, and had close connections with the Mercers Company. He died in 1503[34] and the Markhall estate passed to his son Edmund. In a letter to his daughter Margaret, More thanks her for letting him know of Shaa's condition. This would appear to refer to Edmund Shaa, as in 1525, the unfortunate young man went insane, and More was made custodian of his property, including the old Ardern home of Markhall.[35] Sir John Shaa, in his will, left bequests to Thomas Rich, and Nicholas Mattock, who was a friend and colleague of Alice's first husband, John Middleton, and was one of his executors.[36] Edmund Shaa died in 1538, and his brother Thomas sold Markhall to Henry Parker, Lord Morley.

More, who got on well with people older than himself, must have admired the daughter of Elizabeth Ardern, who was a few years his senior, meeting her not only on his visits to Essex, but also as the wife of a prominent Mercer. He had many dealings with the Mercer's Company in a legal capacity. He rented his first matrimonial home, the Barge, at Bucklersbury, from them. It was the property of the Hospital of St Thomas of Acon, the Mercer's headquarters. He was made a Freeman of the company in 1509, just before John Middleton died.

Sir Andrew Dymoke died in 1508, making Alice's mother, Elizabeth, a widow for the third time.[37] She acted as his executor, as she had done for the estates of her other two husbands, accumulating a large fortune in land from them all.

She certainly outlived her son-in-law, John Middleton, as there is a reference to her dealings with tenants on estates near Colchester, in 1510.[38] Alice's mother was well known for her forceful character and talkative ways, characteristics that she passed on to her daughter. She probably died in the early days of Alice's marriage to More. The distinctive ornament she is wearing in the brass at Latton Church appears to be identical with the oval medallion with pendants that Alice is wearing in the Holbein painting of the More family.

Having traced the fortunes of the Markhall estate of the Arderns, which Sir Peter Ardern left to his eldest daughter, Anne, we look at his estate at Enfield.

These include Enfield Chase, held under the Duchy of Lancaster, which had previously been a Bohun property.[39] This he left to his younger daughter Elizabeth. But the Arderns' close association with the Tudors lost them the property, and in 1483, on coming to the throne, Richard III transferred the lease to the Duke of Buckingham. Enfield is still the property of the Duchy of Lancaster. There is an entry in the *Feet of Fines* for Essex, of More and his brother-in-law George Colt purchasing property in Enfield in 1527, adjacent to the land once held by the Arderns.[40]

Alice's first husband, John Middleton, was a man of considerable standing and importance. To be a Merchant of the Staple of Calais implied that he had great financial resources to call on, as he was dealing in large quantities of merchandise for import and export, under a licence from the Crown. From the mid-fifteenth century these merchants had been limited to thirty eight at any one time.

John Middleton's will was made on 4 October 1509, and was proved on 11 November of that year. Its contents give us some idea of his comfortable situation, the extent of his property, and his devotion to Alice.

After recommending his soul to Almighty Jesus, to the Virgin Mary and all the Company of Heaven, he states that he wishes to be buried in the Church of St Katherine's Coleman, before the image of St Katherine in *'the high quire'* of the church. This church, which was situated close to the Tower of London, just escaped the ravages of the Great Fire of London in 1666, but was pulled down and entirely rebuilt in 1734. This new building was itself pulled down in 1923.[41] All that is left of the place where Dame Alice's first husband was buried is a little courtyard, with a plaque to mark where the church stood, and an evocative smell of sweet herbs and spices from a warehouse nearby, where the delicious aromas from their preparation hangs on the air, as it did in that part of the city in Tudor times.

His friend and fellow Mercer and Merchant of the Staple of Calais, Nicholas Mattock, was co-executor of his will, with Alice. Mattock has already been mentioned in connection with the will of Sir John Shaa. Like John Middleton he owned property in Hitchin, and built the south porch of the church, where the arms of the Staple of Calais can still be seen. Middleton also owned property in Yorkshire, and left money for the church at Eastrington, in the county of Howden. Agnes Middleton left money to the same church in her will in 1474, which is in the records at York.[42] And she can be found in the pedigree of the Middleton family as John Middleton's Aunt.

John came from the branch of the Middleton family that owned Stockeld

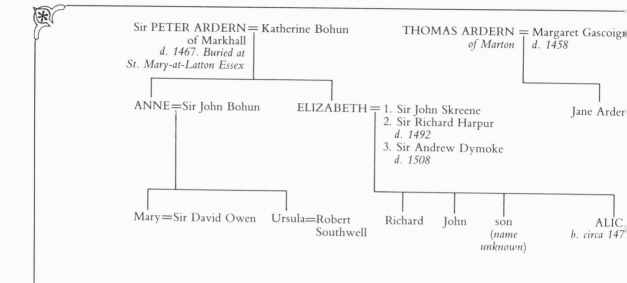

Sir PETER ARDERN = Katherine Bohun
of Markhall
*d. 1467. Buried at
St. Mary-at-Latton Essex*

THOMAS ARDERN = Margaret Gascoign
of Marton   *d. 1458*

ANNE = Sir John Bohun

ELIZABETH = 1. Sir John Skreene
2. Sir Richard Harpur
d. 1492
3. Sir Andrew Dymoke
d. 1508

Jane Arder

Mary = Sir David Owen   Ursula = Robert Southwell   Richard   John   son (*name unknown*)   ALIC. *b. circa 147*

Alice = 1. Thomas Elrington
d. 1563   *d. 1523*
2. Sir Giles Alington
d. 1586

Arms of Ardern of Essex
and Yorkshire

The relationship between Alice and John Middle

Park, Yorkshire.[43] The Middletons and Arderns both owned property in Yorkshire within a few miles of each other. Sir Peter Ardern's land was at Bishop Wilton Easewold and Hoxby, and his brother Thomas Ardern at Marton.[44] Alice was, in fact, related to John Middleton by marriage. He was the son of John Middleton, Mercer and Merchant of the Staple of Calais, and Agnes Creyke. Agnes' brother Thomas Creyke had married Jane Ardern, daughter of Thomas Ardern of Marton, Sir Peter Ardern's brother.[45] Thus from the pedigree shown above it can be seen that Elizabeth Ardern, Alice's mother, and John Middleton's aunt, Jane Creyke, were first cousins.

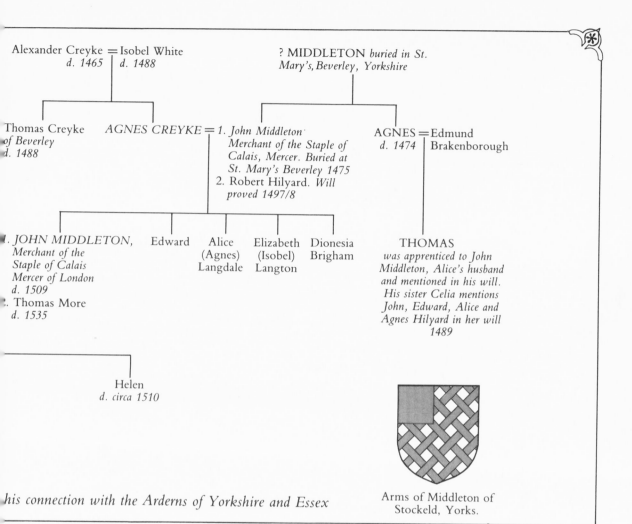

Alexander Creyke = Isobel White
d. 1465 | d. 1488

? MIDDLETON *buried in St. Mary's, Beverley, Yorkshire*

Thomas Creyke
of Beverley
d. 1488

AGNES CREYKE = 1. *John Middleton Merchant of the Staple of Calais, Mercer. Buried at St. Mary's Beverley 1475*
2. *Robert Hilyard. Will proved 1497/8*

AGNES = Edmund
d. 1474 | Brakenborough

1. JOHN MIDDLETON, *Merchant of the Staple of Calais Mercer of London d. 1509*
2. *Thomas More d. 1535*

Edward

Alice (Agnes) Langdale

Elizabeth (Isobel) Langton

Dionesia Brigham

THOMAS *was apprenticed to John Middleton, Alice's husband and mentioned in his will. His sister Celia mentions John, Edward, Alice and Agnes Hilyard in her will 1489*

Helen
d. circa 1510

his connection with the Arderns of Yorkshire and Essex

Arms of Middleton of
Stockeld, Yorks.

Stockeld Park, which is in the West Riding of Yorkshire, still stands today, although the main body of the house was rebuilt by James Payne in 1763. The house has extensive grounds with large woods of oak and chestnut, and stands in a high position on the north side of a hill. The arms of the Stockeld Middletons appeared on the tomb of Alice's daughter, Alice Alington and her husband Sir Giles Alington, in Horseheath Church, Cambridgeshire. The Middletons were staunch Roman Catholics throughout the penal times. In spite of crippling fines they managed to remain at Stockeld until the 1880's.

Alice's two daughters, Alice and Helen, were both alive at the time of their father's death, in 1509, as they are mentioned in his will. But as Alice only took her elder daughter to live with her on her marriage to More, the younger daughter must have died some time between her husband's death, and her marriage to More in 1511.

Apart from a few religious bequests, and a dowry of £100 each for his two daughters if they reached marriageable age, he left his entire fortune to Alice for her life, and after her death, to be divided equally between his two daughters, or the whole estate to the surviving daughter. Thus Alice inherited a large estate from him, making her a very eligible widow. Both the Middletons and the Mores had property in Hitchin. From a description of part of the Middleton estate that Lady Alice sold in 1536, one of their properties in the town stretched from Bridge Street and the old Priory to the south, as far as the rectory manor to the west, and as far north as Bancroft Street.[46] This is a considerable area of the old town, as those who are familiar with Hitchin will realize. In 1504, More and his father, Sir John, purchased an interest in a third of the manor of Charlton, just south of this property of the Middletons.[47]

The town of Hitchin in 1826 / reproduced by kind permission of F. Ballin.

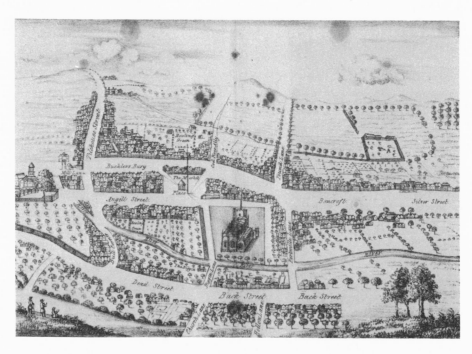

We have seen that the hastiness of More's marriage to Alice is readily accounted for as Alice, was, in fact a member of a family that were near neighbours of Jane Colt's family, a woman More had known for many years. More had many good reasons for wanting Alice as his wife. For all his spirituality, More followed the ordinary worldly standards of the era in which he lived, when advantageous marriages for yourself and your children were considered as necessary, for instance, as sending your children to the right school and university are today. He took great care to see that his own family made good marriages. He brought suitable wards into his household, whose fortune and station in life were above his own, and married his children to them.

Alice, as an heiress of the Ardern family, and widow of John Middleton would certainly have come up to the high standard of wealth and family connections that More sought for his family. He would also have admired her as a competent housewife and mother, and as an amusing companion. Alice had been widowed less than two years when Jane More died, and Cresacre More suggests that she was, at the time, being sought after in marriage by a friend of More's, who asked More to help him with his suit, probably because More knew her so well. With the usual mixture of unkindness mingled with wit with which so many tales of Dame Alice are told, Cresacre recounts the episode:

> *'I have heard it said that he wooed her for a friend of his not once thinking to have her for himself; but she wisely answering him that he might speed if he would speak on his own behalf. Telling his friend what she said unto him, with his own good liking he married her, and did that which otherwise he would perhaps never have thought to have done.'*

Cresacre now goes on to give his biased opinion of the case:

> *'And indeed her favour as I think, could not have bewitched or scarce even moved any man to love her, yet she proved a kind and careful stepmother to his children.'*[48]

But Alice does seem to have moved one man to love her, for she had already been married and given birth to at least two children, and been left her husband's entire estate for her life as well as being made his executor. John Middleton certainly seems to have loved her. That More was in such great haste to marry her as soon as the opportunity arose was surely because as a shrewd judge of character, he wanted to make sure, in spite of criticism and competition, that he should secure for himself a remarkable lady, whom he had known for much of his life, to be his wife, companion, mistress of his household and stepmother to his children.

Mistress Alice Middleton's second husband, Thomas More / The Kylin Archive.

Mistress Alice More

'it is even better to rule than be ruled'

LIKE ALL stepmothers-to-be, Alice must have given a great deal of thought to what her new role would entail in the few hours between More's nocturnal visit to Father Bouge, and their wedding on the following Monday.

She was bringing her considerable fortune with her as well as her daughter, Alice, aged about ten years. More was still distressed by the death of his first wife, as were their four small children. Jane was only twenty three years old when she died. All of us who have taken on the task of becoming a stepmother, which includes taking over the household as well as the children, will agree that it is a great advantage if the previous wife has been known, and better still, loved. Alice had known Jane as a near neighbour in Essex, all her life, and, as by all accounts she was a lovable person, had been fond of her. Competent housekeeper and devoted mother that she was, Alice took over the management of More's household at the Barge with skill. It was her husband's learning, and the cleverness of her eldest step-daughter Margaret that could have daunted her, as well as the intellectual visitors to the house. More's three daughters showed, at an early age, their skill in academic studies that was later to make them renowned in Europe. Alice felt herself more at home with the little boy, John. More said of this fourth and last child that his wife had so prayed for a boy, and now had one that would be a boy all his life. Indeed a friend of the family, said he was no better than an idiot. This was, however, in comparison with his clever sisters, for More says of him later that *'He liked his towardly carriage'*. Even the hypercritical Erasmus styles him a young man of great hopes. His courage was never in doubt, and on refusing to take the Oath of Supremacy after his father's death, he was imprisoned in the Tower. Mistress Alice's own daughter, Alice, was not only very beautiful, but was also highly intelligent, and was looked upon by More as one of his most successful pupils.

Jane Colt had been rather overwhelmed by More in the early days of her marriage to him. In fact things were going so badly, that More took her home to Netherhall to see if her father could help them sort out their difficulties. Alice was made of sterner stuff, and quite a match for More with his teasing and sometimes domineering ways. She waged a lifelong battle with him to improve his wordly position. In this she had some powerful relations behind her. Her cousin's kinship with Henry VIII through the Owen Tudors, and the Southwells' close friendship with Henry VII, gave an added reason for her wishing to get him into Court circles. It is interesting to speculate on the possibility that if More had not married Alice, he would never, in fact, have embarked on the public career which ultimately lead to his downfall. The quieter life of a lawyer and scholar were far more suited to his temperament and inclinations.

Alice, like many wives, made many attempts to smarten up her husband's appearance. The careless way he wore his gown, untidily hitched up over one shoulder and imitated by some of his most ardent admirers, annoyed her very much. Although her ambition to see him as a prominent member of the Court was realized, she was unable to prevent him setting off to see the King in his carpet slippers.

We catch a glimpse of her lively, dominating mother in a conversation with More late in their marriage, after her mother's death.

'What will you do,' she complains to him one day, *'Will you sit by the fire and make goslings in the ashes with a stick as the children do?'*

'What would you do, I pray?,' comes the patient reply. More must have known quite well what the answer was going to be, but, as usual was enjoying the fun.

'By God' says Alice, *'Go forward with the first; for as my mother was wont to say, God have mercy on her soul, it is ever better to rule then be ruled. And therefore, by God, I warrant you, I would not be so foolish to be ruled where I might rule.'*[49] More must have heaved a sigh of relief that Alice's mother, Elizabeth Ardern, had gone to God, and that he only had the daughter to contend with. A mother-in-law of the same calibre would have tried even his saintly patience.

'By my troth,' he replied, *'In this I dare say you speak truth for I never found you wanting to be ruled yet.'* In this encounter, More definitely had the last word. It was said that her greatest fault was that she would, now and then, show herself to be her mother's daughter *'kith after kind';*[50] but as the narrator who wrote under the pseudonym of Ro. Ba. says in his *Life of More, 'It is of their nature to be a little talkative'*. Alice was well aware of her reputation for being sharp-tongued, and was used to More teasing her about this side of her character. In writing about

wives to his friend Cranvelt he said:

*'As to what you write about ill-tempered wives, I am so far of your opinion that
I do not think it possible to live with the best of wives without some discomfort.
. . . This I would say with all the more confidence were it not that we generally
make our wives worse by our own fault.'*

Some perceptive comments about Alice come in Dr Elsie Hitchcock's notes
on Roper's *Life of More*, *'Roper never acquainted his readers with More's first wife's
death or the marriage to the second'*.[51] On the other hand, Father Bernard Bassett, a
descendant of More through Margaret Roper, tends to soar into the wilder
realms of fancy to explain away, to Alice's detriment, why More married again,
and so soon after Jane's death, and, oddest of all, why he married a widow older
than himself; as if this was freakish happening. He even goes to some lengths to
emphasise the side of More's character that had once made him wish to become a
priest, and assumes that he married the most physically unattractive woman he
knew, to help him keep some secret vow of celibacy!

If Erasmus's assessment of it is right, the portrait that Hans Holbein drew of
her is a lifelike one, and even in her fifties, Alice was a personable looking lady.
If she looked as charming as this in her fifties, she must have been even more so
fifteen years earlier when she married More. On one aspect of her character all
More's biographers agree, that she was an extremely efficient housekeeper, and
stepmother to his children. After having had his household at the Barge taken
over by her, he found that untidy as he was himself, his home became more
orderly, giving him more time to pursue all the vital aspects of his varied and
complicated life. After his legal work was done for the day, he would come
home to spend as much time as he could with his wife and children. He wrote to
Petrus Aegidius:

*'I come home, and commune with my wife, chat with my children and talk with
my servants. All these things I reckon and account as business, for as much as
they must be done, and done must they need be, unless a man will be a stranger
in his own house. And every man must do his utmost to be civil and obliging to
those whom nature had provided to be companions of his life, or chance, or
choice, and yet not spoil them by too much condescention, or by foolish
indulgence turn his servants into masters.'*[52]

Dame Alice found visitors like Erasmus and Ammonio, Henry VIII's Latin
secretary, long outstaying their welcome. She felt that they dominated More's

free time, time which she thought should be spent with her and the children. Erasmus, before Alice came to the Barge, had actually stayed a year with the family, an unconscionably long time for any guest to be around. That More enjoyed Alice's company enormously, shines through the descriptions of their early married life and this pleasure continued right to the end. She was not overwhelmed by his great learning and saw that his home was run to fit in with the wonderfully varied facets of his profound and spiritual character.

Alice's new husband was much in favour of stepmothers. He already had one himself, and was a devoted stepson. His father, Sir John More, married at least three times. More's mother, Agnes Graunger, was dead before 1507, and by the time of his marriage to Alice, his father had certainly embarked on his second marriage, to Joanna Burton. More was always delighted with his father's choice of stepmother for him. Again, Erasmus, writing to Peter Giles, a mutual friend, writes:

'It would be difficult to find any one living on such good terms with their mother as More does with his stepmother. For his father has brought in one stepmother after another, and he has been as affectionate with each of them as with his mother. He has already introduced a third, and More swears that he never saw anything better.' [53]

He greeted the last, Alice Clarke, formerly Alice More, sister of Sir Christopher More of Looseley in Surrey, with great delight. This was her second marriage, and she is mistakenly described in the Gollancz edition of Roper's *Life of Sir Thomas More* as being Alice Middleton.[54] More would have enjoyed the mistake of thinking that he had married his own stepmother! Much as he welcomed his father's marriage at the age of seventy, it was because his last stepmother outlived his father, that More did not, in fact, inherit the family property of Gobions, at North Mimms, in Hertfordshire. The estate lay between North Mimms on the west, and Northaw to the east, and extended as far north as Essenden and Hatfield. The possession of such an estate would have greatly relieved the financial worries that overtook him in his retirement from the King's service, as Lord Chancellor. Much as Alice worried about their finances, we never hear sharp words about the fact that it was a stepmother that kept More out of his inheritance. Henry VIII sequestered the property from Alice More, senior, and it was restored to Anne Cresacre by Queen Mary, on the death of John More, in 1547, although the family did not return to live there until early in the next century.

The Barge, at Bucklersbury, near the Poultry, was within the shadow of Old

St Pauls. This enormous cathedral which had the longest nave in Europe, 100 feet longer than the Cathedral at Milan, with a spire higher than Salisbury, dominated the Mores' life until they moved to Chelsea. Bucklersbury with its narrow winding streets of small shops, selling every kind of herb and curios, was a claustrophobic place for the country-bred Jane Colt when More brought her there as a bride. But Alice had lived in London as the wife of a silk merchant for many years, and its surroundings would have held no strangeness for her. We are so used to looking at the More family as painted in Holbein's family group at the house in Chelsea, that we tend to forget that More spent nearly twenty years of his life at the Barge, and Alice fourteen, and that only ten years of his life were spent at Chelsea, the last three of them with his disgrace, and towards the end, the threat of death hanging over them.

The roar of traffic drowns the sound of ghostly voices that might be heard near the site of the Old Barge, Bucklersbury. Queen Victoria Street has slashed its way across the narrow road. The large timber and stone building took its name from the barges that came up to the wharf nearby. It was the last house on the south side of the street, and looked directly across at the Mores' parish church, St Stephen's, Walbrook. If it stood today it would command a good view of the Mansion House. It was the property of the Hospital of St Thomas of Acon. Originally More leased only part of it, but by 1513, because of the increase in the size of his household and his improved financial position, he had the lease of the whole building. In 1954, near the site of the Barge, and probably under its garden, during the digging of the foundations for a new building, a temple of Mithras was discovered. It was left on view to the public for a short time, before the concrete jungle took over again. More, with his love of curiosities, would have enjoyed this remarkable find in his own front garden.

'*As sweet as Bucklersbury in simple time*' was Shakespeare's description of the district of the City of London where Thomas and Alice More lived for so long. Although there is no description of the house as early as 1511, there is a fairly comprehensive account of it as it was during the time of the Clements, who took it over from the Mores, and were their tenants. It appears in the account of a case bought by John Clements against Dr Alban Hill who occupied the house while the Clements were in Louvain, and also against Sir John York, who seized a great deal of the contents during their absence.[55] The more permanent fittings and furnishings of the house were probably the same as during the More residence there, as of course the arrangement of the rooms.

In the garden were three fair herbaries, and a great cage for birds worth £10, obviously part of the Mores' famous menagerie. The house contained a Great

Hall, a gallery, with a chamber next to it, and a maid's chamber. There was a *'great study'* with a closet beside it, and the Great Chamber had a little chamber within it. There was, of course, a Chapel and also a summer parlour, kitchens, laundry, larder, and stables, all with small chambers leading out of them with beds. Such permanent fittings as the *'great cupboard of wainscote',* with four gold escutcheons, in the Hall; the lead gilt dial in the gallery; the *'great press'* to hold three hundred books, and the *'partition of wainscote with laten and joined work'* would have been contemporary with the Mores. The great crucifix and divers images in the chapel may also well have been the same, as More refurbished the chapel at Chelsea when he moved there. The *'great hanging crapel'* in the Court is rather a mystery but sounds a fairly permanent fixture.

The hospital of St Thomas of Acon was situated just beyond the west end of Bucklersbury, at the junction of the Poultry and Ironmonger's Lane. It was used as the headquarters of the Mercers Company, and it was here that Erasmus would take himself off to stay, when, having outstayed his welcome, he became weary of the carping tones of Mistress Alice. He once wrote to Ammonio *'I am bored with England, and More's wife is bored with me.'*[56] He must have been a very difficult guest, E. M. Routh writes:

> *'He was often out of health and spirits, could not bear the smell of fish, could not bear beer, but was a connoisseur of wine, and wanted salads mixed with oil and vinegar the French way, and never bothered to speak English.'*[57]

Alice, having successfully got him out of the house, had not come to the end of her troubles with him; like many absent-minded guests he was liable to leave some of his belongings behind, which had to be returned to him. He even complained, at one time, of More not returning his property, a book, as speedily as he would have wished. More had picked it up, read it, and then forgotten to send it on to him.[58] Erasmus was full of complaints of any hospitality he received in England, and even the two years spent at Queen's College, Cambridge, were not greatly to his liking, so that his dissatisfaction with the hospitality as dispensed by Mistress Alice was not surprising. Certainly More never pressed him to stay when he threatened one of his hasty departures.

After More's marriage to Alice, one of the first children to increase the number in the Barge household, apart from Alice's own daughter, was the three year old Anne Cresacre. More may have been prompted to acquire her wardship by a practical suggestion from Mistress Alice, who knew of the child through the Yorkshire relations of her first husband, John Middleton, or the Arderns. Anne was the only child of a wealthy landowner, Edward Cresacre.

His estate at Barnborough was near Eastrington, mentioned in the Middleton wills. She was born in 1511, and by the time she was two, both her parents had died. She came into the More family a year later. She was a lively, light-hearted little girl, and a great joy to Mistress Alice, sharing her love of beautiful clothes and jewellery. Her enchanting face gazes down at us from Holbein's incomparable drawing of her, made for the family portrait, so unhappily destroyed by fire in the eighteenth century. She was, herself, quite a tease, even laughing at More's hair shirt that she spotted on a hot summer day, much to the annoyance of the owner.

To purchase the guardianship of a ward of court was a favourite form of investment. The guardianship continued until the child was twenty-one if a boy, and sixteen if a girl, and the guardian had complete control of the ward's property until he or she was of age. In Anne Cresacre's case the arrangement was

Anne Cresacre / by gracious permission of Her Majesty the Queen.

of great mutual benefit. She had the caring love of this remarkable family, and married More's only son John when she was eighteen, in 1529. Her husband and their children benefited by her great wealth, which was to be their chief means of support after More's attainder and death.

More, as previously mentioned, became the guardian of Edmund Shaa, the owner of the Ardern property of Markhall, due to his insanity, in 1525. More purchased two other wardships during his marriage to Alice. One was that of Giles Heron, the son and heir of Sir John Heron, Treasurer of the Chamber; Giles married More's youngest daughter Cecily in 1525, three years after entering his household. In 1527, More purchased the wardship of John Moreton, another wealthy landowner, who had become insane. More's understanding of people who were mentally sick, and his ability to help them, may have been his reason for such harrowing assignments. Although a man of More's high principles would never have abused his position as a guardian, many wards found themselves in cruel hands, and during the Protectorate, such wardships were finally made illegal. In one case of such abuse, Giles Alington, More and others came to the defence of Jane Colt's first cousin, Dame Alice's son-in-law, Thomas Elrington. He was the son of Simon Elrington, and on his father's death being still a minor, had become the ward of Sir Thomas Lovell. They brought an action over income due to him from lands inherited on the death of his father. [59] Sir Thomas Lovell, who had been Surveyor of the Court of Wards, died on May 2nd 1524, a year after Thomas Elrington's death. In his will he clearly wished to right the wrong he had done to his ward, and requires:

'Restitution to be made to Sir Thomas More, executor of Thomas Elrington, Giles Alington and his wife (Alice) late wife of Elrington, for the profits of the lands taken by Sir Thomas Lovell during Elrington's non-age.' [60]

Thomas Elrington had married Mistress Alice's daughter Alice in 1516, thus adding another link to the close relationship between the Colt family and the Mores.

Of the four stepchildren that Mistress Alice acquired on her marriage to More, the six-year-old Margaret was the most like her late mother in looks, and had inherited her father's intellectual ability, and she was therefore perhaps the hardest of the children for Alice to understand. From her early childhood her father had coached her in Greek and Latin, and she was to become one of the most learned women of her day. Alice, knowing her own limitations as a scholar, was determined to take advantage of More's desire to teach her an instrument and to sing. Erasmus has to admit that she proved a conscientious and apt pupil, he writes:

'It was a striking achievement . . . To persuade a woman, middle-aged and set in her ways, and much occupied with her home, to learn to sing to the cithern and lute, the monochord, or the recorder, and to do a daily exercise set by her husband.' [61]

Encouraged by these excellent results, More rather rashly went on to try and teach her science. In this field he was far from successful. He writes with rueful humour of Mistress Alice's attempts to become a scientist. [62] Placing a globe in front of her, he tried to explain how the earth was the centre of all things, and therefore how the centre of the earth is the lowest spot in creation, from which everything ascends in every direction. He went on to say that if a millstone were dropped through a hole bored right through the centre of the earth, from one side to the other, it would fall to the centre and then stop, if it went beyond the centre it would be falling upwards from a lower place to a higher. This was too much for the practical Mistress Alice. More continues in the third person:

'Now while he was telling her this, she nothing went about to consider his words, but as she was wont in all other things, studied all the while nothing else but what she might say to the contrary. And when he had, with much hard work, and oft interrupting, brought his tale to an end: "Well" quoth she "I will argue like, and make you a sample. My maid hath yonder a spinning wheel – or else because all your reason resteth on the roundness of the whorls – come hither girl, take out your spindle, and bring me hither the whorl. Lo, sir, you make imaginations I cannot tell you what. But here is a whorl which is as round as the world is. And we shall not need to imagine a hole bored through, as it hath a hole bored through indeed (Alice is certainly one up on More here), *but yet because ye go by imaginations, I will imagine with you.*

Imagine me now that this whorl were ten miles thick on every side and this hole through it still, and so great that a millstone might go through it. Now if the whorl were stood on end, and the millstone thrown in at the other, would it go no further than the midst? I trow you, by God, if one threw in a stone no bigger than an egg, I ween if ye stood in the nether end of it, five miles beneath the midst, it would give you a pat upon the pate, that it would make you claw your head, and yet should ye feel none itch at all?" '

Amidst much laughter the sphere was put away for good, but the sweet sounds of More and his wife playing duets continued. Eramus said that the first six years of his marriage to Mistress Alice, before the pressure of being the King's servant weighed him down, were the happiest in his life.

The School

'*The reward of wisdom is too solid to be lost like riches*'

ALTHOUGH MISTRESS ALICE's attempts to emulate her husband and step-children were strictly limited to the sphere of music, she was as anxious as More himself that these clever children should take every opportunity to absorb all the learning that he was so anxious to impart. No headmistress of a great girls' school could have been more conscientious than Mistress Alice in ensuring that a strict routine of study was adhered to. Erasmus wrote to Budé in 1521:

> '*His wife whose strength lies in mother-wit and experience rather than book learning, controls the whole institution with remarkable skill, acting as a kind of overseer who gives each one his task and sees that she performs it, and allows no idleness or frivolous occupations. . .*'[63]

The '*School*', as it was called, was modelled on More's *Utopia,* and More taught the children himself until 1516 when, owing to pressure of work, he had to give it up and appoint outside tutors for them.

It was in 1516 that Alice's daughter, Alice Middleton, married Jane Colt's cousin, Thomas Elrington. His grandfather, Sir John Elrington had been a distinguished Treasurer to the household of Edward IV, Constable of the Tower, and Minister for War. His eldest son Symon was the father of Thomas. This first son-in-law of Dame Alice was a wealthy young landowner, with property in Hertfordshire, Yorkshire, Middlesex and Kent. His largest estate was at Denecourt, Brenzett, near Romney Marsh, in Kent, but they divided their time between the Willesden property, in Middlesex, and the house at Hitchin, in Hertfordshire.[64] This was situated near to some property owned by Alice, by the Priory gates, probably in Bridge Street.[65] Erasmus, in a letter of 1521, gives a glowing description of Alice's daughter and her young husband.[66]

Erasmus, a great friend of More's / The Kylin Archive.

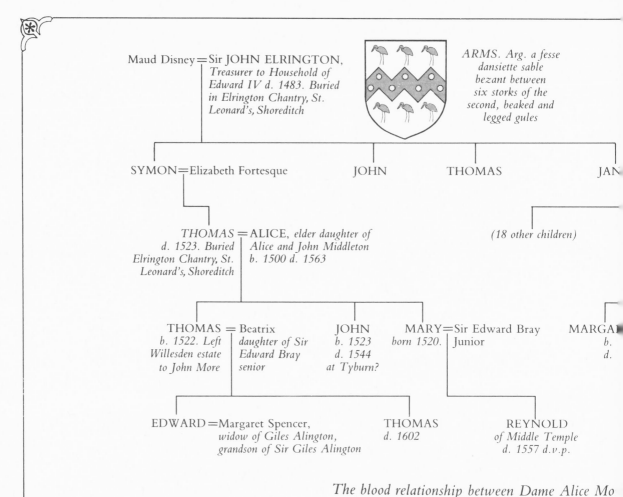

Maud Disney = Sir JOHN ELRINGTON, *Treasurer to Household of Edward IV d. 1483. Buried in Elrington Chantry, St. Leonard's, Shoreditch*

ARMS. *Arg. a fesse dansiette sable bezant between six storks of the second, beaked and legged gules*

SYMON = Elizabeth Fortesque   JOHN   THOMAS   JAN

THOMAS = ALICE, *elder daughter of* *d. 1523. Buried* | *Alice and John Middleton* *Elrington Chantry, St.* | *b. 1500 d. 1563* *Leonard's, Shoreditch*

(18 other children)

THOMAS = Beatrix   JOHN   MARY = Sir Edward Bray   MARGA *b. 1522. Left* | *daughter of Sir*   *b. 1523*   *born 1520.* | *Junior*   *b.* *Willesden estate* | *Edward Bray*   *d. 1544*   *d.* *to John More* | *senior*   *at Tyburn?*

EDWARD = Margaret Spencer,   THOMAS   REYNOLD *widow of Giles Alington,*   *d. 1602*   *of Middle Temple* *grandson of Sir Giles Alington*   *d. 1557 d.v.p.*

The blood relationship between Dame Alice Mo

Whatever his feelings may have been for the mother, there is no doubt about his great admiration for the daughter:

> '*He also has a stepdaughter of great beauty and exceptional gifts, married for some years now to a young man not without education, and of truly golden character*'.

Mistress Alice must have been well-pleased that her daughter had married such a delightful and prosperous young man. The couple had three children; Mary, the eldest, was born in 1520, Thomas in 1521, and John in 1522. They

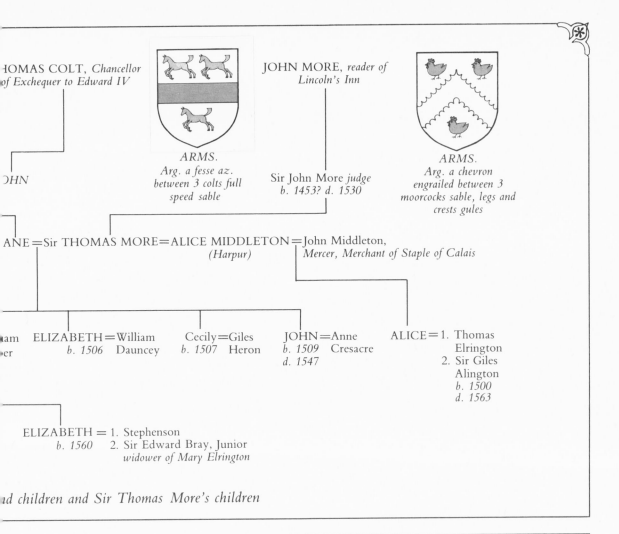

THOMAS COLT, *Chancellor of Exchequer to Edward IV*

JOHN MORE, *reader of Lincoln's Inn*

ARMS.
Arg. a fesse az. between 3 colts full speed sable

Sir John More *judge*
b. 1453? d. 1530

ARMS.
Arg. a chevron engrailed between 3 moorcocks sable, legs and crests gules

JOHN

ANE = Sir THOMAS MORE = ALICE MIDDLETON = John Middleton,
(Harpur)   *Mercer, Merchant of Staple of Calais*

am
er

ELIZABETH = William   Cecily = Giles   JOHN = Anne   ALICE = 1. Thomas
b. 1506 Dauncey   *b. 1507* Heron   *b. 1509* Cresacre   Elrington
                          d. 1547   2. Sir Giles
                                          Alington
                                          b. 1500
                                          d. 1563

ELIZABETH = 1. Stephenson
b. 1560 2. Sir Edward Bray, Junior
           widower of Mary Elrington

ad children and Sir Thomas More's children

were the first grandchildren to come to the Barge at Bucklersbury. Through this marriage, Alice's grandchildren, and More's four children became second cousins, with Sir John Elrington as their mutual grandfather, and a close bond of friendship grew up between them.

By 1516, Margaret More was eleven years old, and the school increased in size with the addition of Anne Cresacre, Margaret Giggs, an unofficial ward, Giles Heron, Joan and William Rastell, More's niece and nephew, Frances Staverton, a daughter of More's sister, and Margaret à Barrow, who married Sir Thomas Elyot. The first tutor appointed was John Clement, who stayed with them until 1518, when he moved into Wolsey's household, and from thence to Oxford, and abroad, to study medicine. He looked after Wolsey as his physician in his last illness, and was doctor to the Royal household. He married Margaret Giggs who also studied medicine, and in 1526 set up home with her in the Barge at Bucklersbury, when it became vacant through More's removal to Chelsea.

The second tutor was William Gunnell, who was a protegé of Erasmus. He was succeeded by Master Drew, probably the Richard Drew who was a Fellow of All Souls, Oxford. Master Nicholas Kratzer, Fellow of Corpus Christi College, Oxford, taught them astronomy. He was particularly interested in sundials, which even Mistress Alice must have appreciated. The last tutor was Richard Hyrde, who was educated at More's expense as he referred to him as *'my singular good master, and bringer up'*. He lived in the house more as a physician than a tutor, as by the time he came into the household, the children were already married. There was a continual stream of young men coming to the house, befriended by More and his wife; one was Master Thomas Pope, who founded Trinity College, Oxford, and another Master Richard Rich whose grandfather had known the Arderns and the Harpurs of Markhall.

More wrote a splendid letter to William Gunnell in 1518, fortunately preserved by Stapleton, laying down the lines he wished the education of the children to follow.[67] Mistress Alice was away from home at the time of this letter, perhaps visiting her daughter and her husband at Hitchin or Willesden. More started the letter by congratulating Gunnell on the excellence of all the children's letters, especially that of Elizabeth *'who shows as much gentleness and self-command in her Mother's absence as would be possible were she present.'* A nice tribute to Alice as a school mistress from her husband. More continues:

> *'Though I prefer learning joined with virtue to all the treasures of kings, yet renown for learning when it is not united with the good life, is nothing else but a notorious disgrace, especially in a woman. Since erudition in a woman is a new thing, and a reproach to the sloth of man, many will gladly assail it, and impute to letters what was really a fault of nature, thinking from the vices of the learned to get their ignorance esteemed as virtue. On the other hand if a woman (and this I desire and hope with you as their teacher with all my daughters), to emulate virtue should build an outwork of even moderate skill in letters, I think she will have more real benefit than if she had obtained the riches of Croesus or the beauty of Helen. I do not say this because of the glory that shall be hers, though glory follows virtue as a shadow follows the body, but because the reward of wisdom is too solid to be lost like riches, or to*

decay like beauty, since it depends on the intimate conscience of what is right,
not on the talk of men, than which nothing is more foolish or mischievous!'

The letter continues in a vein to which Mistress Alice, and her little ward Anne Cresacre, turned a blind eye, both being extremely fond of fine clothes and adornments:

'Warn my daughters to avoid the precipices of pride and haughtyness, and to
walk in the pleasant meadows of modesty; not to be dazzled at the sight of gold;
not to lament that they do not possess what they erroneously admire
in others; not to think more of themselves for gaudy trappings, nor less for
want of them; neither to deform the beauty nature gave them by neglect,
nor to try to heighten it by artifice; but to put virtue in the first place, learning
in the second, and in their study to esteem whatever may teach them piety
towards God, charity to all, and Christian humility in themselves'.

Both Mistress Alice and Anne Cresacre got the better of More over the adornments, and in the family portrait by Holbein all the girls are splendidly dressed, in the height of fashion. The mistress of the house had been at work there. When Anne first asked More for a billement of pearls, he offered her one of peas, but this is another battle Alice won, and Anne is wearing just such an ornament in her portrait.

One of the school's more light hearted lessons was learning the Greek alphabet by shooting at the letters with a bow and arrow, a delightful contrast to the fairly arduous task that was set them by their father of writing to him every day that he was away from them, in Latin. While he still had his legal practice, and slept at home most of the time, this task did not occur very frequently. But after the great success of a mission he went on to Flanders in 1515, when he was away from the family from May to October, the correspondence began in earnest, supervised by Mistress Alice, who made sure that the letters were sent off daily.

In 1516 he became a frequent visitor at Court, and after winning a case for the Crown involving a Papal ship, he was asked to join the King's service. In 1517 he became a full member of the Court as Master of Requests. As usual Erasmus and Mistress Alice reacted quite differently to the new appointment, and consequent rise in his fortunes. She was delighted with his advancement, but Erasmus said it was a great loss to learning. More himself said he was as uncomfortable at Court as a bad rider in the saddle.[68] Much of his time was now spent with the King, and he only managed to get back to The Barge for about two nights a month. During this time the members of the household moved about a great deal, and all Mistress Alice's powers as an organiser were called into play. While the family home was still in the City of London, frequent visits were made to More's father, Sir John More, out at Gobions – his property in Hertfordshire two miles south east of North Mimms, which he acquired in the reign of Henry VII. The house was pulled down in 1836 by the owner of the adjoining property, Brooklands, and only a folly arch gateway remains. But the grand staircase was taken to a house nearby called Hook, which was largely built from material of Gobions.[69]

In a letter to Margaret, Cecily and Elizabeth, More compliments them on the good continuance of their studies, in spite of all the moving about. He writes:

> *'I cannot express my dear children, the deep pleasure your eloquent letters give me, especially as I see that although travelling, and frequently changing your abode, you have not allowed your customary studies to be interfered with, but have continued your studies in logic, rhetoric and poetry.'*[70]

On receiving a batch of their letters while staying at Court, More especially commends John for his efforts and writes:

> *'There was not one of your letters that did not greatly please me; but to confess frankly what I feel, the letter of my son John pleases me best, both because it was longer than the others, and because he seems to have given it more labour and study. For he not only put his matter neatly and composedly, in fairly polished language, but he plays with me both cleverly and pleasantly, and turns my jokes on myself wittily enough, and this he does not only merrily, but with due moderation, showing that he does not forget that the is joking with his father, and that he is cautious not to give offence at the same time that he is eager to give delight.'*[71]

In John, Mistress Alice must have found more of a kindred spirit than in the girls, for although he had a lively wit, he was certainly not the scholar that his eldest sister had become.

Mistress Alice and Anne Cresacre were inclined to take their teasings of More a little too far. Neither of them had time for More's austerities, and as we have seen, Anne, on catching sight of More's hairshirt one hot summer afternoon, laughed heartily at it. It was Margaret, not Mistress Alice, who used to wash it for him, and she knew of the knotted chords with which he used to whip himself. It was largely due to the balanced influence of Alice, who refused to countenance these excesses, that the household did not drift into a semi-monastic establishment, but remained to the end a comfortable family home.

Alice's lack of deep spirituality was treated light-heartedly by herself, and her husband. On returning from the confessional one day, having been well shriven, she baited him with:

'You can be merry, because I have finished with past naggings, and now intend to start all over again!'

More always accepted her teasings in good heart, but was delighted to get his own back at her over her attempts to improve her personal appearance. Erasmus reports:

'Among other things, when he divers times beheld his wife what pains she took in straight binding up her hair to make her a fair, large forehead, and with a straight bracing in her body to make her middle small, both twain to her great pain, for the pride of a little foolish praise,' he said to her, *"Forsooth, madam, if God give you not Hell, he shall do you great wrong, for it must needs be your own of very tight, for you buy it very dear, and take very great pains thereof."'*

Erasmus then went on to say of their relationship:

'He lives on such sweet and pleasant terms with her, as if she was as young and lovely as anyone can desire, and scarcely any one obtains from his wife by masterfulness and severity, what More does from his by blandishments and jests.'[72]

Mistress Alice, like Jane Colt before her, was very short of stature and when More was asked why he married short women, he answered:

'Wote you not that women were necessary evils? Then do I follow the Philistine's rule who wills us of two evils to take the lesser, so do I of my wives.'[73]

In 1518 when Margaret More was 13, William Roper joined the household at The Barge, on his admission to read for the Bar at Lincoln's Inn. He was to prove a difficult problem for Alice, as a future stepson-in-law. They lived in close proximity to each other for sixteen years, but in his *Life of More* he refers to her seldom, and then with little charity. He saw all of her faults, and few of her virtues, and there was, as so often happens in families after a death, much trouble between them when Alice became a widow. He disliked her sharp tongue, which must have been a sore trial to his rather slower wits. Roper was devoted to More, but was often quite unable to understand his train of thought, although he admitted that he used to pretend to do so. This was quite unlike Mistress Alice, who if she failed to catch a point, said so without hesitation.

Four years after Roper's arrival at The Barge, on being called to the Bar in 1521, he married Margaret. He was a well-off man, inheriting considerable property from his father, in particular the large house at Well Hall, in Essex, which became their main home. Soon after his marriage he became a great admirer of Luther, and the lengthy arguments he had with his father-in-law, with, no doubt, Mistress Alice putting in a word now and then, geatly upset the household. Roper used to get extremely angry from time to time. More finally said to Margaret, *'I will no longer argue and dispute with him, but will clean give him over, and get me another while to God, and pray for him.'* [74] Much to the family's relief, shortly afterwards, Roper returned to the Faith.

After these arguments were over, there were further heated disputes over the King. Roper remarked how lucky they were to have a monarch who was such a staunch Catholic, and when More told him he could see doubts arising on that score, Roper angrily disagreed. It was obvious that Roper could sometimes be as uncomfortable company as Mistress Alice.

During 1518 and 1519, when he was made a Privy Councillor, More accompanied the Court, acting as Royal Secretary, and in 1520 attended the King to the Field of the Cloth of Gold, where he would have met Sir Giles Allington, cupbearer to the King, and father of the man who was to become Mistress Alice's second son-in-law. In 1521, much to Alice's delight her husband was made Under Treasurer of England, and knighted, and she became the Lady Alice More. Erasmus wrote of the event in a letter to Budé in 1521:

'More is to be congratulated. He neither aimed at or asked for it, but the King has promised him to a very honourable post, with a salary by no means to be despised: he is to be Prince's Treasurer. This office in England is in the first rank of grandeur and distinction, but it is not unduly exposed either to unpopularity or to the tedious press of business. He had a rival for it, a fairly influential man who wanted the office so badly that he would not object to holding it to his own cost and charge. But that admirable King gave him the clearest proof of his high opinion of More, in that he went so far as to give him a salary when he did not want the post, rather than accept an official who did not need to be paid. Not content with that, this most generous Prince has also knighted him, nor can there be any doubt that some day he will honour him with yet greater distinction when the occasion presents itself; for normally with yet greater distinction when the occasion present itself; for normally Princes

show a much greater tendency to promote bachelors. But More is so deeply imbedded in the ranks of married men, that not even his wife's death has given him his freedom. For having buried his first wife, who was a girl when he married her, the widower has now taken unto himself a widow.' [75]

The field of the Cloth of Gold, June 1520 / The Kylin Archive.

Lady Alice More

'mutual affection of minds'

JOHN MORE was seven years old when his stepsister Alice married Thomas Elrington, his second cousin, who was in his mid-teens. Elrington had been the ward of Thomas Lovell, who held the appointments of Chancellor of the Exchequer, Constable of the Tower, and Surveyor of the Court of Wards.[76] During the next seven years the older boy was to become devoted to John. The Elringtons had three children, Mary, Thomas and John, and Alice was expecting her fourth child when her husband fell ill in September 1523, and died before the child was born. There were in fact, only three children of the marriage, so young Alice must have lost this fourth child. Thomas Elrington stated in his will that he wished to be buried with his ancestors at *'Hoggeston'*.[77] This was the area of London now known as Hoxton, and is adjacent to Shoreditch. Thomas's grandfather, Sir John Elrington, Treasurer to Edward IV, founded a chantry in St Leonard's Church, Shoreditch, and was buried there. There was no other church in Hoxton before 1826, so Thomas must have been buried in the Elrington Chantry in St Leonards.

Dame Alice and her husband had been very fond of this young man and his tragic death at such an early age was a great sorrow to them. In one of his last letters from the Tower, More mentions with love and affection this young man of *'golden character'*, Lady Alice's first son-in-law, who died in his early twenties.[78] More had taken a great interest in him and his affairs. It seems, indeed, that young Elrington had a post under More in the Treasury, judging from an entry book, preserved in the Treasury Records at the Public Record Office:

> *'For Sir Thomas More, Knight, Sub-Treasurer of England, a certain payment per year pro rata of the time, at £173.6s. per annum owed from May 2nd, of XIII year (Henry VIII) until the Feast of Michaelmas following year, by the hands of Thomas Elrington, Teller.'*[79]

Lady Alice, a painting after Hans Holbein the younger, formerly at Corsham Court.

Thomas Elrington made More one of his executors, his wife being the other. He made his will on 23 September 1523, and died before the end of the year. His daughter Mary was three, Thomas two, and John one year old. He showed his great devotion to John More by stating in his will that if none of his own children survived to maturity all his property, after his wife's death, was to go to him. In fact all three children did reach maturity. The contents of his chief house at Hitchin, which goods *'Sir Thomas More, Knight, Under Treasurer of England, lately gave to him'*, were bequeathed to his wife, as well as a life interest in his estates in Kent and Sussex, which included the Manor of Denecourt. Thus Dame Alice's daughter found herself, at the age of twenty-two, a considerable heiress. A year later she married for the second time, into the Alington family.

The Mores were already well acquainted with Sir Giles Alington who, in 1522 at the age of twenty two, had inherited his father's title and estate of Horseheath in Cambridgeshire. More's father, Sir John More, was one of Alington's Trustees, before he came of age.[80] He was first married to Ursula Drury, who bore him one son, Robert. She died in 1522, the same year as his father, and in 1524, young Sir Giles became the second husband of Alice Elrington. He proved to be a staunch and loving son-in-law to Dame Alice until the end of her life.

She and her husband must have visited Horseheath Hall, and it is worth looking back into the records of the house to get some idea of the large establishment of which Alice Alington became mistress, and where Dame Alice's grandchildren were brought up. The earliest mention of the Alington family being in possession of the house was in the will of William Alington in 1446. Before then the house was held by the Audley family, under the Earls of Richmond.

It was through the marriage of the second William Alington to Elizabeth, daughter of Sir John Argentine, that the office of cupbearer to the King at his coronation came into the family. Elizabeth, and her sister Joan, were co-heirs of their father, and the office was inherited from him. The magnificent collection of silver and gilt cups, ewers and bowls which the young Alice found at Horseheath were largely presents from reigning monarchs to their cupbearer at coronations, weddings, and other Royal occasions. The name of Argentine is still carried on in the Alington family, one of the distinguished descendants being Cyril Argentine Alington, Headmaster of Eton, and Dean of Durham, 1872-1955.

The park at Horseheath was originally about 320 acres, but Sir Giles increased this by about 400 acres. There were forty heraldic shields in the mansion, twelve of them in the parlour, ten in the great Hall, and eighteen in the chapel. There was considerable stable accommodation, and a large coach house. In addition to these there was a doghouse, a dovehouse and a farm. There was a stately avenue of elm trees, mentioned by John Evelyn in his diary.[81]

Although nothing remains today of Horseheath Hall, the site of the house can still be seen. It is reached by travelling about a mile out of the village to the east, when a steep drive to the left leads to Horseheath Park Farm. Following a track past the farm house across a field and over the old ha-ha, the visitor comes to Hall Meadow, a windy exposed hillock, which commands a wide view of Horseheath to the west, and faces the blustering, cold winds from the east. There were two cedar trees, one at each end of the house, which marked its exact position. These have recently been cut down, but Acre Pond, named for its size, can still be seen. Its ancient brick walls are covered with brambles and weeds, but it is still fished for roach, tench, rudd and carp by the boys from the

Horseheath Hall, a view from the west /
reproduced by kind permission of Dr. and Mrs Dawson.

village. The old garden pond can be seen in the grounds of the present farmhouse.

When the house was rebuilt in 1665, some of the great state rooms were left as they were, including a set of rooms on the first floor, facing south, which included the parlour, a withdrawing room, and a bedroom, suitable for the *'Lady's distempers and lying in',* it was here that Dame Alice's nine grandchildren were probably born.

Meanwhile the household at the Barge, that had been More's home for twenty years, had increased in size. More's three daughters were getting married, and the first grandchildren arriving. These facts, added to the growing importance of More's position, led them to decide to move from The Barge to something larger. In 1523 More leased Crosby Place, which consisted of a Hall, and a group of tenements. Preferring the idea of building a house in the country, at Chelsea, More sold the lease of Crosby Place to his good friend Bonvisi, a silk merchant, of Italian origin, from Lucca. Antonio Bonvisi remained a lifelong friend of More and his wife, and they enjoyed a great deal of good hospitality from him. As well as being a trader in wools, silk and jewellery, he was a great patron of learning, so that they both in their various ways enjoyed his company enormously, Alice in discussions of his merchandise, which would have taken her back to the days when she was a silk merchant's wife, and More, of course over the latest books he had acquired.

Both More and his wife loved talking, and More, in his *Dialogue of Comfort,* gives a vivid description of a supper party conversation, at Bonvisi's house:

'Her husband (More himself), *had much pleasure in the manner and behaviour of another honest man, and kept him, therefore, much company, by the reason whereof he was, at his meal time the more oft from home. So happened it on a time, that his wife and he together supped with that neighbour of theirs, and then she made a merry quarrel with him, for making her husband so good cheer out a-door, that she could not have him at home. "Forsooth, Mistress" quoth he (as he was a merry dry man). "in my company nothing keepeth him but one; serve you him with the same sauce and he will never be from you"'*.

"What gay thing may that be" quoth she.

"Forsooth Mistress", quoth he, *"Your husband loves well to talk and when he sitteth with me, I let him have all of the words".*

"All the words" quoth she, *"Marry, that I am content, he shall have all the words with goodwill, as he hath ever had. But I speak them all myself, and give*

them all to him, and for ought I care for them, so shall he have them still; but otherwise, to say that he shall have them all, you shall keep him still, rather than he get the half!" [82]

Alice, as usual, must have caused much laughter at such parties.

Amongst the many city friends that Alice and her husband had in common, one of the most well known was the merchant, Richard Fermor. He was a merchant of the Staple of Calais, a Master Grocer, a dealer in silks, and had been a colleague of the late John Middleton. In 1514 he was mentioned as a co-plaintiff with More, and Thomas Mattocks, a kinsman of Nicholas Mattocks who had been executor of John Middleton's will, and friend of Alice's father, Richard Harpur, in the purchase of some property in Essex, the manor of Mardites. [83] In 1513, and again in 1515, at the request of Henry VIII, he was given permission by Margaret of Savoy to export from Flanders huge quantities of wheat and wool. [84]

There is an interesting record of him in the Warden's accounts of the Grocer's Company for 1519, when at the Livery dinner on July 16th five lady guests were invited. They were his own wife and one of her kinswomen, the Lady Semer, and Mrs More and her daughter, Alice Elrington, who was about twenty-one at the time. The menu for the meal sounds delicious. The first course consisted of *'Capon rostyd, pyke and Venyson bake; the second Quayles roasted, Fresh Salmon, Tarte, followed by wafers and Ipocras;* (a filtered cordial drink, made of wine flavoured with spices). [85]

In 1910 the Hall of Crosby Place was moved, stone by stone, from the City to Chelsea, and it now stands by the river, at the corner of Danvers Street, near the site of More's Great House. A very imaginative garden has been made, betwen the Hall and Chelsea Old Church, called after William Roper, with a special area for the use of dogs, a touch that would have appealed to the animal loving Dame Alice.

Just before the Mores move to Chelsea, Elizabeth and Cecily More were married at a double wedding to William Dauncey and Giles Heron. Bishop Tunstall, who had given permission for More to marry Dame Alice, *'with no banns asking'* also gave his permission for a double wedding, in a private chapel. Although the licence states that it was to be held in the Alington Chapel at Willesden, Middlesex, [86] this was actually the Elrington chapel, part of the estate of the late Thomas Elrington, and by then controlled by his widow, Alice Alington. Yet again the children in the family were marrying well. William Dauncey had estates in Hertfordshire and Buckinghamshire. Giles Heron inherited estates in Essex, Rycote Manor, Oxfordshire, and Shakerwell Manor,

Hackney, where much of their time was spent.

Although the children and in-laws were frequent visitors to the family home, by 1524 all of them except John and Anne Cresacre had large establishments of their own. More continued as Anne's ward, managing her estates up in Yorkshire until her marriage to his son in 1529.

Erasmus, in describing the great success of More's second marriage in his letter to his friend Budé, show great understanding of the quality and strength of their remarkable partnership:

> 'What makes wedlock delightful and lasting is more the goodwill
> between mind and mind than any physical passion, so that far stronger
> bonds unite those who are joined by mutual affection of minds as well,
> and a wife has more respect for a husband whom she acknowledges as
> a teacher also. Devotion will not be less because there is less unreason in it . . .
> I differ profoundly from those who keep a wife for no purpose except
> physical satisfaction, for which half-witted females are better fitted.
> A woman must have intelligence if she is to keep her household
> up to its duties, to form and mould her children's characters,
> and meet her husband's needs in every way.'[87]

The Great House At Chelsea

'a beautiful and commodious residence'

ALTHOUGH there is still some argument as to the exact situation of the Mores' house at Chelsea, it is generally supposed that it stood about six hundred feet back from the river Thames, on its north bank, and originally had a frontage of some 164 feet. It would have straddled across what is now Beaufort Street, from east to west. The King's Road was to the north, then a quiet country lane leading to Fulham Palace, and Old Church Street was to the east. The building, with Henry's financial assistance, was built in a remarkably short space of time. At the time of More's Attainder, nine years later, he still had some outstanding debts to the King for this loan. The original property purchased by More, in

A reconstruction of St Thomas More's house at Chelsea, from the earliest known plans by J. Symands 1595 / by kind permission of Monseignor Shanahan.

1524, for the site of his new house, was a farmhouse on land now occupied by numbers 90-100 Cheyne Walk, which at some time was known as Lindsey House. The property had enjoyed the right of feeding cattle on the common from time immemorial. At the same time as his purchase of the farm for the site of his house, he bought more land at Chelsea and across the river at Battersea. The building of the house began in 1524, and was completed in 1525.

The parish church, of which More had the living, was to the south-east corner of the estate. He added a side chapel to the existing structure for his household, and a vault to act as a family mausoleum. In the east window of this chapel are the arms of the More family, and the epitaph that More wrote for himself on his retirement can still be seen in the chancel of the main chapel. Jane Colt's body was removed from its grave in St Stephen's Walbrook, and placed in the new vault, and it was here that More wished to be buried, with Dame Alice. It is in this epitaph shattered by a bomb in an air raid in 1941 as mentioned before, but beautifully restored, that More paid his tribute to Dame Alice as a stepmother. Knowing well the bad reputation that stepmothers had in general, and perhaps thinking, quite rightly, that descriptions of her from such friends as Ammonio, and his own teasing comments, were an unfair tribute to such a remarkable lady, he has put his words there for posterity, and indeed for all who visit Chelsea to see. The epitaph, written in Latin, was translated as follows by William Rastell, More's nephew:

> 'Here lies Jane, dear little wife of Thomas More, who intends this tomb for Alice and me. The first united to me in my youthful days, gave me a boy and three girls to call me father. The second, a rare distinction in a stepmother, was as affectionate as if the children were her own. It is hard to say if the first lived with me more beloved than the second does now. Oh how blessed if fate and religion had permitted all three of us to live together. I pray the tomb and heaven may unite us, thus death could give what life could not give.'

It is good to know that Dame Alice must have had the pleasure of seeing this public tribute to her made by her husband; a worthy reward for all her efforts over the comfort, care and consolation of him and his family. When the bomb fell on the church on the night of 16-17 April 1941 the official record related that *'rising out of all the ruin, almost incredibly, stood the More Chapel, the pillars with the Holbein capital supporting the arch, intact, unscathed.'*[88]

The arms of the Colts, argent a fesse azure between three colts full speed sable, bring to mind a charming gesture made to his son-in-law by Jane's father John Colt. He left More in his will, in 1522, the delightful legacy of *'a present of one of his best colts, at his own pleasure.'*[89]

All the travelling to and from the Great House was done by barge, manned by liveried watermen. From Chelsea it plied down river to Westminster and the city, and sometimes Greenwich Palace, or up the river to Hampton Court. The landing stage was at the bottom of the garden and was reached through a wicket gate. Here the family would often stand and wave goodbye to More on his way to the Court, wherever it happened to be.

For the first seven years of their life at Chelsea, More was away a great deal of the time, attending on the King, and left the running of the household and farms in Dame Alice's capable hands. The permanent residents there at this time, apart from More and Dame Alice, were John More, Anne Cresacre, Giles Heron, who assisted Dame Alice in the running of the estate, and Cecily his wife, More's secretary John Harris and his wife, formerly Dorothy Colley, Henry Pattenson, the fool, and numerous servants. Because of the Barge's proximity to Lincoln's Inn, the Ropers spent much of their time there, with John Clement and his wife, formerly Margaret Giggs. The Clements had set up house there in 1526, as tenants of More and Dame Alice, who still owned the lease.

It was in the autumn of that year that Hans Holbein was sent to the More household by Erasmus, to paint the family portrait. A careful study of it shows that Dame Alice had little of the *'beaked-nosed harpy'* look of Ammonio's description. The eyes are set wide apart, and the mouth has a sweetness about it, with a humorous tilt at the corners, which is wholly delightful. The beautiful drawing by Holbein in the British Museum of an unknown gentlewoman, reproduced on page 121, once thought to be Margaret Roper, but now repudiated as such, has a strong resemblance to Dame Alice about the eyes and mouth, and may in fact be Alice Alington, Dame Alice's daughter. So greatly admired by Erasmus for her dazzling beauty, she must have been drawn during Holbein's stay with the family, and would have been about twenty-nine years old.

Cecily and John have inherited their father's looks, although John has rather a weak chin. It was no doubt Dame Alice's doing that in the portrait they are all extremely well dressed, some extravagantly so. Alice was keeping up the tradition of the women of the Ardern family, who loved to dress in the height of fashion, as seen on the Harpurs brass at Latton. The incomparable original sketches for a large painting, so sadly destroyed by fire in 1752, are in the Queen's collection at Windsor, and the original composite sketch was sent to Erasmus, and is now in the Museum at Basle. Even if the painting had not been destroyed, as it was executed in water colour, it had already badly deteriorated the last time it was seen.[90] The oil painting of Dame Alice copied from it is not an original Holbein, (see page 49). Once in the possession of Lord Methuen, at Corsham Court, near Bath, it has now been sold; the latest enquiries have traced it to Switzerland. The Nostell Priory version, owned by Lord St Oswald, is probably the original, and is still in his house in Yorkshire.

On receiving the sketch of the family group, Erasmus wrote of his delight in it, and draws attention to the extraordinarily good likeness of all the sitters which Holbein has caught. On 5 September 1529, three years after the picture was completed, he wrote to Margaret Roper:

> *'I cannot find words to express the delight I felt when Holbein's picture*
> *showed me your whole family almost as faithfully as if I had been*
> *among you. I often wish that before my last day, I may look even*
> *once more on that dear company to which I owe a great part of what ever little*
> *fortune or glory I possess, and to none could I be more willingly indebted.*
> *The gifted hand of the painter has given me no small portion of my wish.*
> *I recognise you all. . . Convey my respectful salutations to the honoured*
> *Lady Alice, you mother; since I cannot kiss her, I kiss her portrait.'*[91]

A close study of the family sketch gives us a delightful insight into their life. Elizabeth stands to the extreme left of the picture, obviously pregnant. Margaret Giggs, next to her, is leaning over old Sir John More, unsuccessfully trying to interest him in a book. His lack of interest in learning must have been a great comfort to his practical daughter-in-law. In later copies of the portrait these two girls have changed places, to bring Elizabeth nearer her father, but the disinterested look on Sir John's face remains.

In this first sketch several of the family, including More, Anne Cresacre, and Cecily Heron, appear to be looking in the direction of Dame Alice, who kneels demurely at a prie Dieu, with her tame monkey, on a chain, clambering up her skirt. This monkey was a great favourite of Dame Alice's, and Erasmus mentions in his Colloquy on Amity, that when this animal was recovering from an injury, it was allowed to walk about without a chain. Was this direction of their heads due to the fact that, when they were arranging themselves for the portrait, Dame Alice was, as usual, directing operations? The note written beside her in Holbein's hand states: *'this one will sit.'* Perhaps as well as organising the family she had complained about her own rather uncomfortable position, on her knees, when the rest of the family were sitting. In the final portrait she is sitting with the monkey quietly beside her, and More has decided to have his small dog at his feet as well. Through all the subsequent changes in later copies of the work, Dame Alice has sadly been removed altogether. In the case of the copy at East Hendred, which is similar to that at Nostell Priory, and nearest to the original, Mr Thomas More Eyston states that her absence from his copy is due to the rotting of her end of the painting by damp. In other versions, as that at the National Portrait Gallery, Dame Alice has been replaced by the male heirs and their wives, looking, in their Elizabethan clothes as if they are in fancy dress. But even in this version, Cecily is still craning her neck round to look at the absent Alice, and Anne Cresacre, Elizabeth, John and More himself look in her direction, as if the kindly but organising voice can still be heard.

The Great House was considerably altered in the late 16th and 17th centuries by subsequent owners, and it is sad that Holbein, while he was in residence there painting the family, did not paint the exterior of the house. He does, however, in the Basle sketch, give us a good idea of what the room looked like in which the family sat for him, full of flowers, books, musical instruments and some animals. There was a weight driven clock on the wall, now in the possession of the Waterton family, direct descendants of John More and Anne Cresacre. The linenfold panelled canopy over the door, and another over the sideboard, and the diamond paned windows, all show that More's house was quite modern for the times, looking more Elizabethan than the earlier Tudor. Dame Alice describes the house herself in a conversation with her husband as *'A right fair house, your library, your books, your gallery, your garden, your orchard, and all other necessaries so handsome about you'.*[92] Alice may have had a special interest in some of More's library, probably inherited through her mother, as the property of her grandfather, Sir Peter Ardern.

When searching through the manuscript drawings in the possession of the Marquis of Salisbury, at Hatfield House, Mr A. W. Chapman suddenly came across two plans, dated 1595, drawn by J. Symands, which undoubtedly relate to the Great House at Chelsea.[93] These are plans of the house as it was at the time Lord Burghley inherited it from Lady Dacre, in 1594, and are of great interest. Four other plans found at the same time are suggested plans for alterations, and bear more resemblance to the drawings of John Thorpe, in the Soane Museum. It was from these plans of Thorpe's made after the alterations, that former speculations about the house More lived in were made, and also theories put forward as to the possible situation of the room in which the portrait was painted.[94]

With the aid of these beautifully drawn plans of Symands it is now possible to make a journey through the old house much as Dame Alice knew it and agree with her that it must have been a fair house indeed.[95]

The front entrance, which faced south onto the river, consisted of a few steps

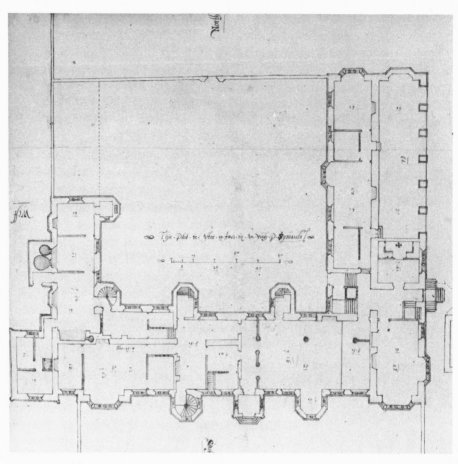

The Great House, Chelsea, ground floor plan by J. Symands 1595 /
by kind permission of the Marquis of Salisbury.

up to a large porch. The visitor was then taken straight into the west end of the
Great Hall, which was seventy-two feet in length, including the dais. The main
body of the hall was entered through a wooden screen, to the visitor's right,
with the entrance to the serving quarters to the left. The dais where the family
would sit was at the east end, protected from the draught from a door in the far
north east corner by another small screen. There was a large fireplace on the
north wall near the dais, similar to the arrangement found in some Oxford and
Cambridge Colleges. There were two deeply recessed windows, one on the
north wall and one on the south, with smaller windows either side. A corridor

The Family of Sir Thomas More from a painting by Hans Holbein / The Kylin Archive.

above the north side of the Hall, on the first floor, supported by pillars, had an oriel window looking down into the hall, and there were also oriel windows at the east and west ends. As can be seen from the design of the Great Hall, there is no position here where the family could have sat to coincide with Holbein's sketch.

Leaving the hall through the door at the north end of the dais, we find the grand staircase on our left. They are wide and shallow, the right hand set probably going down to a cellar below. The left hand flight go up to a half landing which has a window facing west. Another few stairs take one to another half landing, with another window facing in the same direction. A few more stairs finally reach the first floor.

Opposite and to the north door of the Great Hall and to the east is the entrance to the Chapel. This is rather small for such a large household, only eighteen feet square, which accounts for the balustrade opening from the room directly above, looking down onto the altar, where Mass could be observed. The altar is on the north wall, and the window here faces east. A. W. Chapman

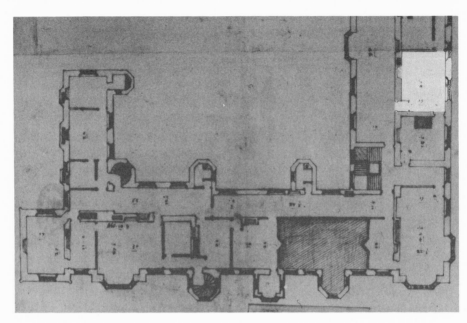

Part of the first floor plan of the Great House, Chelsea, showing the room whre Holbein painted the More family / by kind permission of the Marquis of Salisbury.

suggested that the portrait might have been painted here, but although the window is in the correct position, the door is not, it would also have been considered quite unsuitable for such a purpose. Near the chapel are a few steps going down into the garden, and in the direction of the New Building which More built later for himself.

On the first floor we have already mentioned the room above the chapel. To the west of this was the long gallery, about eighty-seven feet in length. It was here that the family portrait hung when completed. It did not have to be taken far from where it was actually painted. The room that fits the sketch is the one that lay directly behind the room above the chapel. It was twenty-six feet long, with ample room for the artist to stand back and examine his work, and nineteen feet wide, large enough for the family to sit down comfortably at the north end of the room. There was a fireplace on the west wall, and, as in the painting, there is a window on the east wall near the door, to the right of the group. From the size of the small figures seen through the open doorway, and the window behind them, they were probably sitting in the far room, which was reached by a short passage with an open balustrade, which could be seen from where the artist was sitting. The rather slight structure of the beams in the sketch indicate that the room was in fact on an upper floor. Any ground floor room would have had heavier beams to support the structure above.

Returning to the ground floor, on the east side, behind the chapel, is a covered cloister, running from north to south. Beside this were several rooms leading into each other, one of which may have been the library. The steps leading to the garden between the hall and the chapel are mentioned by More's great nephew, Father Ellis Heywood:

> 'It is a beautiful and commodious residence, to which when fatigued with his occupation in the city he returned for refreshment and solace of retirement. After dinner, one descends about two stones throw onto the garden, walks on a little lawn in the middle, then up a green hillock, where one halts to look round. It is an enchanting spot, as well from the convenience of the situation – from one side almost all the noble city of London being visible, and from the other the lovely Thames, being crowned with almost perpetual verdure and covered with lovely flowers, and the sprays of the fruit trees so admirably spaced and interwoven, that looking at them they appear like a veritable piece of living tapestry made by nature herself, so much more noble than the works of art, as she gives fuller satisfaction than that imitation of beautiful things, which leaves the mind more dissatisfied than content.'[96]

The charming irregularity of the east wing of this early house, so obviously planned for the use of this particular family, gives us an entrancing glimpse into the life of the household. Most of this wing was pulled down, and replaced by a plan of greater symmetry, but less charm. After hanging the family portrait in the gallery, More asked the King to come and look at it. He was so impressed that he immediately commissioned Holbein to paint the royal portraits, thus putting him on his way to fame and fortune.

It has always been assumed that Henry VIII's informal visits to the Chelsea household were made solely out of his devotion and admiration of More himself, and as a very strange thing for him to do, humbling himself as it were, to speak with the likes of Dame Alice. As the granddaughter of Sir Peter Ardern, Alice was, in fact a kinswoman of Henry, her first cousin Mary Bohun being his aunt, and her other cousin Ursula being married to one of Henry VII's greatest friends, Robert Southwell. Henry, therefore, on his informal visits to Chelsea, was not only dropping in to see a friend, but also one of his relations.

Dame Alice and her husband shared a great love of animals. Alice was particularly fond of them as household pets, whereas More had a great curiosity about their behaviour, and loved to study their habits. Amongst their menagerie they had apes, monkeys, weasels, ferrets, rabbits and of course dogs. Like all dog lovers, Alice's heart went out to any stray animal, and Ro. Ba. tells us of an incident when this delightful trait in her character led her into trouble:

> 'Dame Alice loved litle dogs to play with. It happened that she was presented with one that had been stolen from a beggar woman. At length Sir Thomas got to hear of it, so caused both his wife and the beggar to come before him in the hall, and said – "Wife come you here, at the upper end of the hall, because you are a gentlewoman, and you good wife stand beneath, because you shall have no wrong." '

He placed himself in the middle, and held the dog in his hands, saying to them:

> 'Are you content that I shall decide this controversy between you concerning this dog? – "Yes" they said. Then each of you call the dog by name and to whom the dog comes, she shall have it. The dog came to the poor woman, so he caused the dog to be given to her, and gave her, besides, a French crown, and desired that she should bestow the dog on his Lady. The poor woman was well paid with his fair speeches, and his alms, and so delivered the dog to my Lady.'[97]

Perhaps this was the same little dog that peeps out from under More's skirts in the family portrait.

In 1529 a disastrous fire attacked More's barns, and Dame Alice sent Giles Heron to see her husband, who was at Woodstock with the King, to tell him the bad news. He immediately wrote to her a letter which is the only correspondence between them that has survived. The barns had been used by poor neighbours in Chelsea, to store corn. His letter throws considerable light on his high opinion of her ability to cope with the crisis, and his belief in her sound, good judgement:

> 'I pray you make good search what my poor neighbours have lost, and bid them take no thought thereon, for I should not leave myself a spoon, there shall no poor neighbour of mine bear no loss by any chance happening in my house. I pray you be with my children and your household merry in God, and devise somewhat with your friends what way were best to make provision to be made for corn for our household, and seed for the coming year; if ye think it good that we keep the ground in our hands, and whether ye think it good that we so shall do or not. Yet I think it were not best suddenly thus to leave it all

*up, and put away our folk from our farm, till we have somewhat advised us
thereon; howbeit if we have more now than we shall need and which can get
them other masters, ye may then discharge us of them, but I would not
that any man were suddenly sent away he wot never whither. At my coming
hither I perceived none other but that I should tarry still with the
King's Grace, but now I shall, I think, because of this chance, get leave this
week to come home to see you, and then shall we further devise
together all things what order shall be best to take.'*[98]

It is good that this practical letter from More to his wife has been preserved. It
not only shows him looking to her for advice, but also shows us their affection
for each other and a close understanding between them. All matters concerning
the Great House, and the large family and friends and servants that surrounded
it, were shared between them, and were their joint concern. More's affection
shines through every mention of her. In a letter to Erasmus he says:

*'My wife desires to send a million compliments, especially for your careful wish
that she may live many years. She says she is the more anxious for
this, as she will then live the longer to plague me!'*[99]

In these happy days, neither of them would have imagined that she, the elder
by seven years, would outlive him by so many.

Although no other letter between More and his wife seems to have survived,
that a continual practical correspondence went on between them while he was
away from home is indicated by More himself, when telling the story of his
servant Davy, the Dutchman:

*'I remember a man of mine . . . Davy, a Dutchman, which had been
married in England, and saying that his wife was dead and buried at Worcester
two years before, while he was in his country and giving her much
praise, and often telling us how sorry he was when he came home and found her
dead, and often how heavily he had made her bitter prayers at
her grave; went about while he was waiting on me in Bruges,*
(in August, 1521), *in the king's business, to marry there an honest widow's
daughter. And so happened it even upon that day when they should have
been made handfast and ensured together, was I advertised from London by my
wife's letter, that Davy's wife was still alive, and had been at my house to see
him.'*[100]

It is cheering to think that while his children were writing him learned Latin
exercises, Dame Alice was keeping him abreast of the family and household
gossip.

The Calm

'*Ever after thy calm, look I for a storm*'
THOMAS MORE

UNDER THE ELTHAM ORDINANCE of 1526 More, as a member of the King's Council, had to wait on him daily. Unless the King gave licence to the contrary, three members, including More, had to attend him at ten in the morning, and at two in the afternoon, not only in case the King wished to confer with them, or ask their advice, but also to hear poor men's complaints on matters of justice.[101] More's name appears amongst those who lodged at the King's house. This arduous assignment kept him away from Dame Alice and the family for most of the time, but it also gave him a first hand opportunity to get to know Queen Catherine of Aragon, with whom he spent many hours. He also had a chance to observe with dismay the King's growing infatuation with Mistress Anne Boleyn.

Before Henry made More Lord Chancellor, in October 1529, he consulted him on the possibility of a divorce from Catherine, who had been unable to give him a male heir to the throne who survived infancy. The King's argument, first put to More in the Great Gallery of Hampton Court, was that his marriage to Queen Catherine was not only against the laws of the Church, but against the laws of nature. To emphasise this point, he drew More's attention to certain passages of scripture. After much thought and deliberation, More made it quite clear to the King that in his view, although Catherine had been married to his late brother, the Papal dispensation that had been given to Henry to marry her was quite valid, and therefore no divorce could be sanctioned by Rome.[102]

More pointed out to the King that this view of the matter was entirely a point of conscience, and begged him to question him on it no more. Henry was devoted to More, and was prepared to accede to his wishes in this matter. More, knowing his master well, foresaw the struggle that lay ahead, and tried to warn

Henry VIII / The Kylin Archive.

his family, in a general way, that in spite of Henry's marked affection for him, if he proved to be a stumbling block to the King getting his own way, all their lives might be in danger. Henry's affirmation that *'he never wished to put any man in a ruffle with his conscience'* were hollow words to More, who knew only too well the vacillating hypocrisy of his master.

Ann Boleyn's jealousy and dislike of More increasingly became a factor in Henry's attitude towards him. She was envious of the King's affection for him, and of his devotion to the Queen, and she looked upon him as a threat to her overwhelming ambition to become Henry's second wife. Although More always made it clear that he would accept any child of such a marriage as being heir to the throne, this was not sufficient for Anne.

More's appointment as Lord Chancellor, the first layman to hold the post for several hundred years, put him in a terrible dilemma. Dame Alice was delighted by such promotion, but More, with his foresight, would have refused the post if he had dared. But Henry was not the man to take no for an answer, so More accepted the office, knowing that if the King persisted with his plans for a divorce, his position as Chancellor and spokesman for the Crown would be untenable.

As Lord Chancellor, More opened what was to be known as the Reformation Parliament in November 1529, and delivered the King's speech.[103] It contained a fierce attack on his predecessor, Cardinal Wolsey, which indicated how much More, by becoming the Chancellor, had put himself in a false position, as mouthpiece for the King. To make such a speech, so lacking charity towards the fallen statesman, would in other circumstances have been out of character. In the early days of his career, More had been on friendly terms with Wolsey, but George Cavendish, Wolsey's servant, in his biography *The Life and Death of Cardinal Wolsey,* makes no mention of him at all. This is strange, as Cavendish was married to Margery Kemp, daughter of William Kemp, of Spain's Hall, Finchingfield, Essex. She was Jane Colt's niece, and therefore related to More by marriage, as well as a neighbour of the Ardens.[104] He either omitted all mention of his master's successor because he disliked him and resented his attack on Wolsey in Parliament, or did not wish at the time he wrote the book to be associated with a man who had been attainted, and executed. Whatever the reason for his silence, it is sad that we have been deprived of a first hand account of the More household by such a skilled writer, and one who must have known them all well.

More had five of his close relations sitting in this Parliament as members. William Roper sat for Bamber, in Sussex; the husbands of Elizabeth and Cecily,

William Dauncey and Giles Heron, sat for Thetford in Norfolk; Dame Alice's son-in-law, Sir Giles Alington, sat for Cambridge, and John Rastell, More's brother-in-law, for Dunheverd now Launceston, Cornwall. These five men, all deeply fond of More, must have been very anxious about his position, in spite of the outward signs of Royal favour, such as the visits by the King to More's home and family in Chelsea. More showed great reticence about talking to his family about the divorce, partly on the principle that the less he said about the matter, the better it would be for his safety and theirs.

As a commoner sitting in the Lords, More's position was unique, the post of Chancellor usually being held by a spiritual lord. Dame Alice hoped that the King would regularise the position by ennobling him, and if he had remained in office longer, this would surely have happened. Henry may have hoped that a lay Chancellor would be more amenable to the idea of a divorce than one who was a cleric. In the early days of the King's *Great Matter,* as it was called, the dispute was basically between clerics, as to whether Henry's marriage to Catherine was valid or not. Only towards the end of More's time as Chancellor did it develop into a struggle which affected clerics and laity alike, a choice between the Pope as supreme head of the Church, or the King.

In December, 1529, Anne Cresacre became the wife of John More. The match was a good one, between two loving, loyal, but not very intellectual people. Although on her marriage Anne ceased to be More's ward, and came into the possession of the Barnborough estates in Yorkshire, she and John, and their children, remained in Chelsea, and there is no indication that they went to live in Barnborough until long after More's death. All her children of this, her first marriage, were born in Chelsea.

In spite of the gathering storm, to outsiders the household at Chelsea appeared very flourishing. In January 1532, before the rift over the marriage forced him to resign, More had still avoided giving his opinion on the King's *Great Matter* openly. He had made the King's speech on the divorce the previous March, and from his silence when asked his own views on the matter, was being gradually forced into an untenable position. In spite of this, he received New Year gifts from the King and Queen of a gilt goblet, and a walking staff wrought with gold, outward signs, at least, that the King still had some affection for him.

During his time as Chancellor he was able to spend more time at home in Chelsea, sitting in the Hall of the house every day, to hear petitions. It was during these sessions that he became so adept at tempering the harshness of the Common Law with equitable solutions, laying the foundation of the great law of Equity, which was finally established in the Judicature Act of 1873.

A daily routine of prayer was drawn up for the household, and Dame Alice, the family and the servants joined him every day in this. After his own private prayers in the chapel in the New Building, the family would assemble for morning prayers together, which consisted of seven psalms, and the litanies. Before he went to bed, he would call them all again together, to go to the chapel near the Hall. On their knees they would say the *Miserere Mei*, a *Salve Regina*, and the *De Profundis*. More also decided that every feast day and Sunday they should all go to the parish church, to hear Mass, and at the solemnities of Christmas and Easter, Whitsun and All Saints, he bade them all get up in the night, and go to church to be present at Matins, which was sung between midnight and daybreak.

Both More and Dame Alice had a great devotion to St Thomas à Becket, and in recognition of this they were both made members of the Fraternity of Christ's Cathedral, Canterbury, in 1530.[105] In December of the same year Sir John More died. Erasmus wrote of him:

> *'More has a father aged, I suppose, not much less than eighty, whose old age is wonderfully green. You could hardly find anyone who carried his years with a better grace. This allows one to hope for a ripe old age for More likewise.'*

More remembers him on his own epitaph, written on his retirement, in 1532:

> *'He was a civil man, pleasant, harmless, gentle, pityful, just and uncorrupted, who having lived to see his son Lord Chancellor of England, thinking himself to now have lived long enough, gladly departed to God.'*

Shortly after his father's death, More came into some of his property, Downes Farm and Waltrapps, at Hatfield. It was three hundred and fifty feet above sea level, and was a considerable estate. It consisted of about 101 acres in Hatfield, and another fifty at North Mimms. From evidence in the Hatfield manorial rolls, Alice was still collecting the income from Waltrapps until her death.[106]

More was, in fact, only Lord Chancellor for two and a half years. He was well versed in the ways of Parliament, having been Speaker in 1523, and had been in close touch with the King and Court for many years, and was well aware of the ill wind that was blowing. There could not have been a worse time for a man with More's strong beliefs and principles to find himself acting as the mouthpiece of Henry VIII. On many great matters that came before Parliament during his Chancellorship, he disagreed totally with Henry; the divorce, the attack on the clergy, and the King's Supremacy of the Church of England.

When, in 1530, an appeal was sent to the Pope on the divorce, More refused to sign it. In 1531 he had to submit Henry's message about the divorce to Parliament, and on 15 May 1532, receive the final submission of the clergy to Henry, as Supreme Head of the English Church. The following day, May 16th, in the garden of York Place, he resigned his office and his career as a statesman came to an end. How far did Lady Alice, with her great ambition for him, and her forceful character, in taking the King's side, persuade More against his better judgement, into taking on the office of Chancellor? The answer will never be fully known, but the part she played in influencing him to do so must have been considerable. Alice's wealth, and her kinship with the King through the Ardern family, would certainly have helped him in his rise to political eminence, and as such would have been welcomed by his children. His scholar friends, such as Erasmus, were very unhappy about his dangerous position in the corridors of power. When the fall came, did his children, with hindsight, partly blame Alice, with her ambition, for leading him into what turned out to be a death trap?

Sanctity may be said to grow in a man or woman out of their reaction to the circumstances in which they find themselves. Dame Alice was certainly a profound influence on the circumstances in which More found himself, and it is arguable that without her he might not have found himself so hard pressed. A London taxi driver once remarked to me on a journey to the More Exhibition at the National Portrait Gallery, that if Henry VIII had not wanted to marry Anne Boleyn, More would never have become a saint. One might add that if More had not married Mistress Alice Middleton, he might not have become a saint.

It was after a service in Chelsea Old Church that it was brought home to Dame Alice, in a poignant way, that More was no longer Chancellor. The custom was for men to sit on one side of the church, and women on the other. During his years as Chancellor, after Mass was over, More would send a servant to his wife, who bowing low to her, would say, *'Madam, my Lord is gone,'* whereupon Alice would gather the female members of the household together, and also leave the church. As usual, he tried to joke with her, and instead of sending a servant, he came himself to the pew, bowed low, and said, *'Madam, my Lord is gone.'*[107] Some biographers cite this as showing how More broke the news to his wife of his resignation, attempting to drive home to her his consequent loss of status. But this surely pays scant justice to her intelligence and standing. She and her husband were accustomed to discuss all practical matters between them, and it is impossible to believe that they had not discussed his possible resignation, and all that it would entail in loss of status and financial prosperity. More did, in fact, forewarn his whole family, before his resignation, of the troubles to come. As Roper put it:

> *'In the time somewhat before his trouble, he would talk with his*
> *wife and children about the joys of heaven, and the pains of hell, of the lives*
> *of the holy martyrs, of their grievious martyrdoms, and their marvellous*
> *patience, and of the passions and deaths they suffered, rather than*
> *displease God; what a blessed thing it was for the love of God, to suffer*
> *loss of goods, and imprisonment, loss of lands, and life also.'*[108]

He had talked about his declining health to many people, including the Duke of Norfolk. His excuse to the King for his resignation was the ever increasing discomfort he was in, due to pains in his chest, caused by stooping over a desk for many hours a day. Poor health was considered to be a valid excuse for resigning office, and More hoped that the King would accept it as such, in his case. Outwardly, at least, it appeared that he had done so, for the first speech that Lord Audley made to Parliament, as his successor, was full of warm praise, and gratitude for his great work as Chancellor. More must have noted with some shame and sorrow what a contrast it was to the one that he had delivered about Wolsey, when in a similar position, less than three years before.

The Storm

'I trust he shall in the stormy seas, hold me up from drowning'
THOMAS MORE, IN A LETTER TO ALICE ALINGTON

L IKE MANY GREAT STATESMEN before and since, More used the first days of his
retirement to write a short autobiography in the form of the epitaph that
was placed in Chelsea Church during his lifetime, and in which he spoke so
lovingly of Dame Alice as his wife, and as a stepmother. He describes his new
position:

> *'More began in his own conceit to wax old, by a certain sickly disposition of*
> *his breast. He therefore, irked and weary of worldly business,*
> *giving up his promotions, obtained at last by the incomparable benefit of his*
> *most gentle prince, (if it please God to favour his enterprise),*
> *the thing from a child in a manner he always wished and desired, that he might*
> *have some years of his life free, wherein he, little by little withdrawing*
> *himself from the business of this life, might continually remember the*
> *immortality of the life to come.'*

More's income as Lord Chancellor was about £140 a year, with the addition
of a further £200 for his position as a Judge in the Star Chamber. He also
received £16 a year for wax, and £64 a year for twelve tunnes of wine. Added to
this he had £100 a year as a Privy Councillor. Legal fees amounted to about
£1000 yearly, roughly half those of his predecessor, Wolsey.[109] In real terms
today, his income free of income tax was about £75,000 a year.

On resigning his office as Chancellor, he still had his salary as a Privy
Councillor, and his rents from his farms in Chelsea and Battersea, and the
manors of Fringford, Doddington, Barley Park and South. He also had the
manor of Downes and Waltrapps in Hatfield.[110] There was Alice's income from
the considerable fortune left to her for her life by John Middleton, and any

ANNE DE BOULEN.

Anne Boleyn / reproduced by kind permission of the Essex Record Office.

74

fortune she had from the Ardern family, although some of this may have already been spent to help maintain the establishment at Chelsea. Bearing in mind that all the children, including Alice's daughter, were well provided for by their marriages, the Mores were not exactly penniless on his retirement, as popular accounts of them tend to make out.

Up to the time of his resignation, the Mores had kept open house for their children and grandchildren. More had never asked them for any financial assistance. But now he and Dame Alice decided that if the children wished to continue to visit them at the Great House in the usual way, they would have to contribute to the housekeeping. What a familiar family predicament they found themselves in, the parents not liking to point out that they were not as well off as they had been and the children so taking the hospitality for granted, that the father is forced to draw attention to the altered situation!

Encouraged by the practical Dame Alice, More sets about tackling the problem in his usual playful way. In the words of Roper:

> *'He called all of us that were his children to him, asking our advice how*
> *he might now, in this decay of his ability (by the surrender of his office so*
> *impaired, that he could not, as he was wont, and gladly would,*
> *bear out the whole charge of them himself), from henceforth to be able*
> *to live and continue together as he wished we should.'* [111]

This was a fairly plain hint that they should offer to pay their own expenses while staying in Chelsea. But Roper, as we have seen, was fairly slow in following More's train of thought, and John not noted for his quickness. Margaret Roper and her sisters, seem also to have been slow to catch More's message. According to Roper's account, not one of them even answered More, let alone immediately offered some money for their keep. By this time, we may be sure, not only was More getting rather embarrassed, but Dame Alice justifiably annoyed. After a long silence, More continues:

> *'Then I will show my poor mind to you. I have lived up at Oxford, at an*
> *Inn of Chancery, at Lincoln's Inn, and also at the King's Court, and so*
> *forth from the lowest to the highest, and yet have I in yearly revenue at this*
> *present little above £100 a year, so now must we therefore, if we like to live*
> *together, be content to become contributaries together. But by my council,*
> *it shall not be best for us to fall to the lowest fare first; we will therefore*
> *not descend to Oxford fare nor the fare of New Inn, but we will*
> *begin with Lincoln's Inn diet, where many right worshipful and of*
> *good years do live full well; which if we do not find ourselves the first*

able to maintain, then we will next year go one step down to
New Inn fare, wherewith many an honest man is well contented.
If that exceeds our ability too, then we will the next year afterwards
descend to Oxford fare, where many grave and learned fathers be continually
conversant, which if our power stretch not to contain neither, then may we yet
with bags and walletts go a-begging together, and hoping that for some
pity some good folk will give us their charity, at every man's door to sing 'Salve
Regina', and so keep good company, and be merry together.'[112]

This conversation was another of More's jokes, as a hint to his children and their husbands that after his retirement as Lord Chancellor he would not be in a position to be as liberal in his hospitality to them all, as he had been at the height of his political career. After all, they all had more than adequate households of their own. As with so many of More's jokes it became magnified out of recognition, to give the impression to future biographers that from the moment of his retirement, he and his wife were practically destitute. The well known but obviously fictitious story of the family going out to collect bracken to burn to keep themselves warm, started by Cresacre More, repeated as fact so often, and portrayed again in Robert Bolt's play *'A Man for All Seasons'*, must be a More jest gone awry. With his own private income from his lands alone, he was still a man of more than adequate means after his retirement, and the question must be asked as to why the myth of poverty was encouraged at this time and continued later by his family. The answer must lie in his fear of an Act of Attainder against him if he refused to take an Oath on the King's *Great Matter.* In these circumstances the less he possessed, the less could be confiscated from him. More would never have been accused of taking bribes after his retirement, if his household had deteriorated so far as to burn bracken to keep warm! As we go on to investigate Dame Alice's position after More's death, not only do we find that the King dealt very lightly with her over the confiscation of More's property, probably because she was his kinswoman, but he was unable to touch her large inheritance from John Middleton, which was in trust for her daughter, nor any fortune left from her own family. But that More was seriously worried about her future, and determined to curtail any unnecessary expenditure is quite understandable.

In spite of the laughter he must have caused in talking to them in this way, the hint was finally taken. There is still no suggestion that they put their hands into their pockets, but as Cresacre More relates *'after this conversation his children went to their own livings, all but my Uncle Roper and my aunt, who lived in the house next to them.'*[113] This was probably the farm house More originally bought (in Cheyne

Walk), where Lindsey House stood later. John More and Anne also remained behind. Their first son, Thomas, was born in 1531, and Austin, their second son, who was Dame Alice's godson, in 1533, after More's resignation.[114]

Having reorganized the family and straightened out the financial position More and Dame Alice settled down to a quiet life in Chelsea, interspersed with visits to her daughter and son-in-law at Horseheath Hall. Alice Alington had nine children by Giles Alington, to add to the three she had had by Thomas Elrington. It must have been a lively household, and one that the Mores enjoyed visiting. Sir Giles also managed their legal affairs for them, and was to prove invaluable in the troubled times ahead. As cupbearer to the King, he was a member of the Court, and so kept them up to date with the news.

On his retirement, More at last had time to settle down to writing, and during the next two years wrote on two subjects close to his heart, the defence of the clergy, and his abhorrence of heresy. The first part of the *Confutation of Tyndale's Answer,* had been published early in 1532, before his resignation. This was followed by a letter to John Frith, against his views on the Eucharist, published early in 1533, and the second part of the *Confutation of Tyndale's Answer.* No one realized better than More that the church needed reform, but from within, not by trying to destroy it from without. Such writers as Frith, Tyndale and Barnes were, according to More, doing the King's work for him in regard to the divorce, and his marriage to Anne Boleyn. Gradually More found himself driven into the position that he so dreaded, that of having to make an open stand in the King's *Great Matter.* In his *Apologie*, published in 1533 a year after his retirement, we find him not only defending his faith but himself.

It was Thomas Cromwell who led the attack on More. It took the form of stating that More had made a lot of money out of combating heresy and defending the clergy. In fact, Bishop Tunstall, then Bishop of Durham, Bishop Clerk of Bath and Wells, and Bishop Veysey of Exeter, had collected the very large sum of £5,000, about £250,000 in present day terms, as a present for him, to show their appreciation of his outstanding service to the country as Chancellor, and his defence of the church against heresy. The prospect of such a sum was greeted by Dame Alice with delight. To her horror More refused it and the Bishops had the wretched task of *'restoring each to their own again.'*[115] It enraged Alice even more that, in spite of refusing such a handsome gift, he was still accused by his enemies of accepting such monies.

In his *Apologie* he makes one of the few references to his financial position at that time, confirming the fact that Dame Alice was still a woman of some substance. Direct reference is made also to the loss he suffered in not inheriting his father's estate at North Mimms, due to the fact that his latest stepmother, Alice More of Loosley, was still alive. In a flash of anger at Tyndale's reference to him:

> '*Covetousness blinded the eyes of that glittering fox,*' More strikes back: '*As for all the land and fees I have in all England, besides the lands and fees I have as the gift of the King's most gracious majesty, is not at this day, nor shall be while my mother-in-law,* (stepmother), *whose life and good health I pray God keep and continue, worth yearly to me living, the sum of fifty pounds. And therefore I have some of my wife, and some of my father,* (whose soul Our Lord assoil),[116] *and some I have purchased myself, and some fees have I of some temporal men . . . I have not had one groat granted me since I first wrote my Dialogue, and that was, ye wot well, the first work that I wrote on these matters.*'[117] More is referring to his *Dialogue of Heresies*.

It is obvious from Tyndale's attack that More's household was still prosperous enough in the eyes of the world to make such accusations feasible, but More, knowing himself innocent of corruption, had good cause to be angry.

The peace of the Chelsea life lasted for nearly a year, and was broken by what seemed to Alice to be a sign that her husband still enjoyed the Royal favour; the invitation arrived for Anne Boleyn's Coronation at Westminster Abbey. The fact that Anne was seven months pregnant at the time, made Henry more than ever anxious to get outward recognition of her as his Queen, and her future child as heir to the throne.

The Bishops Tunstall, Clarke and Gardiner paid another visit to More, this time to beg him to accompany them to the ceremony, and assist at it, offering him twenty pounds for the purchase of a new gown. He accepted the money for the gown, but refused the invitation! Dame Alice was bitterly disappointed, for not only did she look on this occasion as an opportunity to re-establish the King's favour, but her son-in-law would be officiating at it, as cupbearer to the King, and her daughter Alice would attend. Some pageants for it had been designed by their old friend Holbein, specially for this occasion.[118] But More was adamant over his refusal, in spite of the Duke of Norfolk's warning that such a refusal would anger the King, and do even more damage to his reputation with Anne Boleyn. But More's love for Catherine of Aragon, as well as his distaste at the idea of giving consent, by his presence to the violation of the sacrament of the Coronation Oath, forced him to take this first public stand against the King's marriage.

'*By the Mass*' said Norfolk, '*it is perilous striving with princes, and therefore I would wish you somewhat to incline to the King's pleasure, for by God's Body, Master More, Indignatio principis mors est.*' More replied, '*Is that all? Then in good faith, there is no difference between your Grace and me, but that I shall die today, and you tomorrow.*'[119]

The conversation at Chelsea continually came round to the fact that if an Act of Parliament was passed on the Succession, and the King's Supremacy, then they must all expect the worst to befall him. '*God give grace that these matters within a while, be not confirmed with an oath,*' was More's constant warning to Dame Alice and the family. Roper, who, as a member of Parliament, was well aware of what was going on, became angry, and Dame Alice,who had a simple solution for salving her conscience in these matters, put the case that it would be quite all right to swear openly, but in her heart say the opposite. It was during these few weeks, before the Act of Succession was passed, that Margaret Roper, so far removed from her stepmother in intellectual prowess and scholarship, drew closer to her over the matter of the oath, seeing clearly, as Alice did, the deadly danger her father was falling into, by taking up such an inflexible attitude. In spite of their many differences, the women of the household were closing their ranks, in an attempt to avert the coming disaster.

It has often been said against Dame Alice that she was totally lacking in understanding of More in his predicament. She was in good company. Not only were More's children in agreement with her over her attitude, but most of the great brains in England. Father Bridgett puts Alice's case well:

> '*To say of Dame Alice that when his time of suffering came she did not rise to the heights of his soul, is merely to class her with nearly all her contemporaries, including almost every abbess, abbot and Bishop in the kingdom.*'[120]

In writing of Alice years later, when their attitude to the Act of Supremacy had changed, Roper and Cresacre More condemned Alice for the very attitude they themselves had taken at the time.

Too late, More tried to settle his property in such a way that Alice would have it, and after her, his children. He appointed twelve trustees, one of them John Clements, to act for the trust on Alice's behalf. At the same time he conveyed the property that the Ropers were living in, to them absolutely.[121] This conveyance was good, and the Roper's Chelsea home was not affected by the subsequent Attainder against More. But the trust for Alice was set aside, and the property was ultimately forfeited to the King. Poor Alice, if her husband had only set these matters in motion directly after he resigned, her position after his death would have been infinitely easier.

The Act of Succession, when it was passed on 30 March 1534, was not quite as deadly as it had appeared in its first draft, whereby it would have been treason and death not to swear to it. Due to a strong lobby in Parliament, amongst whose number one would have hoped to find More's sons-in-law, and supported by Lord Audley, the offence for not swearing was changed from treason to misprision of treason, which carried imprisonment, and forfeiture of property, but not death. It was due to this that More and Fisher survived another year.

Members of Parliament had to swear to the Act first, and the blow that all had been waiting for in the household at Chelsea quickly followed. It was on the 12th of April the first Sunday after Easter, that More and Roper set out to go to St Paul's to hear the sermon, and afterwards walked across to the familiar old house, The Barge at Bucklersbury, to see John and Margaret Clements. The conversation must have been concentrated on the new Act, and its consequences, and have touched also on the transference of More's property to Dame Alice. The news that he was in the city reached the Council and thus it was in his old home that he received the summons to appear before the Lords at Lambeth, to take the Oath, the following day.

On hearing the news, More immediately returned to Dame Alice at Chelsea, and spent the rest of the day trying to make arrangements with her for the care of the house and servants, if he should not return. She made a last desperate attempt to see if some loophole could be found, that would enable him to swear to the Act with a clear conscience. Roper in one of his most moving passages in his Life of More, describes what was to be for More his last morning in Chelsea, and the last time Roper saw him:

> 'Then Sir Thomas More, as his accustomed manner was always, ere he entered into any matter of importance, as when he was first chosen for the King's Privy Councillor, or when he took any weighty matter upon him, would go to church and be confessed, and hear Mass, and be houseled (take communion); so did he likewise in the early morning, the selfsame day that he was summoned to appear before the lords at Lambeth. And whereas he ever more used, before at his departure from his wife and children, who he tenderly loved, to have them bring him to his boat there to kiss them all, and bid them farewell, then would he suffer none of them forth of the gate, to follow him, but pulled the wicket after him, and shut them all from him with a heavy heart, as by his countenance it appeared, with me and our four servants there, took he his boat towards Lambeth. . . wherein still

sitting sadly awhile, at last he suddenly rounded me in the ear, and said,
– Son Roper, I thank Our Lord, The field in won. What he meant
thereby, I whist not, yet loath to seem ignorant, I answered, – Sir,
I am therefore very glad.'[122]

That spring of 1534 was a very warm one. After More's first refusal to take the oath, while Dame Alice and the family waited anxiously at home in Chelsea, he sat in a small room overlooking the gardens of Lambeth Palace, watching with a mixture of amusement and consternation the faces of the clerics walking outside on the lawn. Those who, like his friend Dr Nicholas Wilson, the King's confessor, had refused to take the oath, passed by the window with grave and solemn faces, on their way to the Tower. Although he was still willing to swear to the Succession, making any children Anne Boleyn might have, heirs to the throne, More persistently refused to swear to the whole Act. The oath as it had been presented to him involved the repudiation of the Papal Supremacy. He stayed with the Abbot of Westminster for five days, and at one time it was hoped that the oath might be rephrased to make it possible for him to take it. But in the end, largely due to Anne Boleyn's persistence, it remained unaltered, and on 17th of April, having yet again refused to swear, More was committed to the Tower.

There is a letter in the Harleian MSS from Cranmer to Cromwell, written the day More was committed to the Tower, suggesting that More and Fisher should only swear to the Act of Succession, making Anne Boleyn's children heirs to the throne, but not to the Preamble which made Catherine of Aragon's marriage to Henry invalid.

Sir Richard Cromwell, nephew of Thomas Cromwell, and great grandfather of Oliver Cromwell, accompanied him there. Dame Alice and his servant John à Wood saw that he was well dressed for his interview with the Lords. On his way to the Tower, Sir Richard begged him to remove the gold chain that he habitually wore round his neck, probably given as a gift from the King when he was knighted. Such articles of value were considered rightful perquisites for the gaoler, and rather than let him have it, Sir Richard wished More to send it back to his wife at Chelsea. This he refused to do. *'I will not'* he said, *'for if I was taken in the field by mine enemies, I would they would somewhat fare the better by me.'*[123] If More had realized how long he was going to remain a prisoner, and what comfort the return of it to her would have given his wife, he might have acted differently.

81

The Prisoner's Wife

'Bon Deus . . . will this gear never be left?'

IMMEDIATELY MORE ARRIVED in the Tower, and before his servant John à Wood arrived with his books and writing materials, he wrote a short letter to Margaret Roper, to let the family know that he was in good spirits:

'Written with a coal by your tender loving father, who in his poor prayers forgetteth none of you all, nor your babes, nor your good husbands, nor your good husbands' shrewd wives, nor your father's shrewd wife most of all, nor our other friends, And thus fare you heartily well for lack of paper.'[124]

Those of us who have visited the Tower tend to see it only across the dark pages of its history, and therefore get a false idea of it during the time of More. Built primarily as a fortress, it was also a Royal Palace, and the gardens were, and still are, pleasant to walk in. It was from the Queen's House that Anne Boleyn set out in triumph to her Coronation, and to the same apartments that she returned, as a prisoner, three years later, in 1536. Like all great houses, and castles, the Tower had its dungeons, but the octagonal room to which More was taken, which can be approached from the Queen's House, now the Residence of the Governor, was soon made comfortable by John à Wood, with coverings on the walls and floor.

Dame Alice had to pay fifteen shillings a week for her husband's keep and five shillings for his servant,[125] equivalent nowadays to about £2,500 a year; not the height of luxury, but quite adequate for More's simple tastes. He writes of an early visit of his wife to him in the Tower. Dame Alice was footing the bill, and, characteristically, she came to critize, but even she was moderately pleased with what she saw. *'She found the chamber'*, More writes, *'mostly fair, and at leastwise it was strong enough* (was this More's joke or hers?). *But with mats of straw, the*

*The Tower of London, taken from a Panorama of London by A.V. Wyngaerde in 1560 /
by kind permission of the Ashmolean Museum, Oxford.*

prisoner had made it so warm, both under foot and round the walls, that in these things for the keeping of his health, she was, on his behalf, glad and very well comforted.'[126]

More then goes on to mention the claustrophobia that Dame Alice felt on entering a prison, when the door was locked behind her:

'But among many other displeasures that for his sake, she was sorry for, one she
lamented much in her mind, that he should have the chamber door
upon him, by night, made fast by the gaoler that should shut him in. "For if by
my trouth, the door should be shut upon me, I ween it would stop my breath."
At that word of hers, the prisoner laughed in his mind, but he
derst not laugh out loud, or say anything to her, for somewhat
he stood in awe of her, and had his findings there much part
of her charity for alms; but he could not but laugh inwardly,
why he wist well enough, that she used on the inside, to shut her
own chamber to her, both door and window too, and used not to open
them all the long night.'[127]

Dame Alice's retort might have been that it is one thing to be locked in a room with the key in your hand, but quite another for the key to be in the hand of a gaoler on the other side of the door. This is the first of many good laughs Dame Alice gave More in the Tower, and it is much to her credit that she was able to amuse him even there.

In these first months in the Tower, More did not have his chamber door locked during the day. He was free to walk in the garden that summer with his visitors, and attend Mass every day, either in the beautiful chapel of St John at the top of the White Tower, or in St Peter's ad Vincula. He and his wife, with their shared love of animals, would have enjoyed visiting the Zoo, which was housed in the Lion Tower, at the south west corner of the fortress. Since 1235, when Henry III was presented with three leopards *'in token of his regal shield of arms'* by Emperor Frederick II, the fascinating menagerie had contained a varied collection of animals, including a white bear, an elephant, and, of course, lions. The zoo remained in the precints of the Tower for six centuries, until 1828, when it was removed to Regents Park.[128]

Although Dame Alice was pleasantly surprised by the comfort of Thomas' early prison days, she would not have run true to herself if she had not, on her first visit, rated him for being so foolish as to find himself there at all. She first reminded him of the beautiful home he had in Chelsea. It would seem from Alice's description of it that, in spite of a few austerities that had been introduced owing to his diminished income, it was still a very comfortable house to live in, and not the bare barracks of a place that we are sometimes led to believe it to have become. She warms to the attack in a charateristic way: *'I muse what in God's name you mean here fondly to tarry.'* She was beginning to fear that he was so peaceful and comfortable in his new abode that he might be loth to leave it. After hearing her awhile, with a cheerful countenance, he said to her, *'I pray thee, good Mistress Alice, tell me one thing, What is that,'* quoth she. *'Is not this house'* quoth he, *'as nigh Heaven as mine own?'* To whom she, after her accustomed homely fashion, not liking such talk, answered *'Tilly Valley, Tilly Valley.'* Nothing was more like his beloved home than a sparring match of words with his dear wife. *'How say you, Mistress Alice,'* he persists, enjoying the fun, *'is it not so?'*

'Bon Deus, Bon Deus, man, Will this gear never be left?'

'Well then Mistress Alice, if it be so', quoth he, 'it is very well. For I see no
great cause why I should have so much joy of my gay house, or of
anything belonging there until, when if I should but seven years lie buried
under ground, and then arise and come hither again, I should not
fail to find some therin that would bid me get out of doors, and tell
me it were none of mine. What cause have I then to love such a house,
as would so soon forget its master?'[129]

More may have been reminding Dame Alice here of the many visits they had made to their old home at The Barge, now occupied by the Clements, and her criticizing the new arrangements, comparing them unfavourably with the place as it was in their own day.

Any wife that makes her husband laugh must be a joy to him. To make a husband laugh after twenty-three years of marriage, as Dame Alice did, is a rare virtue; to continue to be able to do so when he is in prison is a triumph of stoutheartedness and courage. There is no record that any other members of the family gave this man, who so loved merriment, the amusement that he obtained from his wife. She rang true in all the good qualities that he loved in her, to the end.

His first great sorrow in the Tower was, in fact, the attempt made by Margaret, his daughter, who wrote to him, in the early days of his imprisonment, to persuade him to submit to the King's wishes, and take the oath. He could sympathize with Dame Alice for constantly pressing him to do this, but he expected better things from his clever, pious child. He had hoped that, of all his family, she would understand and sympathize with the stand he was making. Her letter came as a terrible shock to him, and caused him much distress. The letter has not survived, but we can gather the content of it clearly from the heart-rending reply:

'If I had not been, my dearly beloved daughter, at a firm and fast point
(I trust in God's great mercy), this good, great while before, your
lamentable letter had not a little abashed me, surely far above all other
things, of which I hear, divers times, not a few terrible towards me.
But surely they all troubled me never so near, nor were so grievous unto me,
as to see you, my well beloved child, in such vehement, piteous manner,
labour to persuade me unto that thing where of pure necessity for
respect unto mine own soul so often given you so precise answer before.
Wherein as touching the points of your letter, I can make none answer,
for I doubt not, but you well remember that the matters that move my
conscience, (without declaring thereof, I can nothing touch the points),
I have sundry times shown you that I will declare them to
no man. And therefore, daughter Margaret, I can in this thing go no
further, but like as you, labour again to follow your mind to desire
and pray you both again to leave such labour, and with my former answers to
hold yourself content.'[130]

He continued on another sad note:

'A deadly grief to me, and much more deadly than to hear of my own death, is
that I perceive my good son, your husband, and you, my
good daughter, and my good wife, and my other good children, and
innocent friends, in great displeasure and danger of great harm thereby.
The let of it whereof, while it lieth not in my hand, can no further
but commit all to God.'[131]

During his time in the Tower, he never tried to influence any of his family not to take the oath. In fact they all did so, except his son John. He must have been deeply worried about the effect that imprisonment would have on the claustrophobic Alice. As long as the offence of not swearing the oath remained as misprision of treason, More knew that although he had temporally lost his freedom, his life was in no danger, and there was even a chance that he might be released. So until the new sitting of Parliament in the November of that year, 1534, his peaceful life in the Tower continued, and Dame Alice was well justified in wondering if he would ever settle down again to the comfortable family life, with all its social and materialistic diversions. The semi-monastic life in the Tower suited her husband too well.

The Council must have been aware of the stalemate that the situation was developing into, for, urged on by Queen Anne, they altered the offence for failing to take the oath from misprision of treason to treason, punishable by death. The blow had fallen. There is no record that More's sons-in-law, stood out against this in Parliament, or that Lord Audley tried to stop it.

More's family and friends, including his old friend, the Duke of Norfolk, knew of his natural dread of physical suffering. In a letter he sent to Alice Alington he writes, *'I counted full surely, many a restless night, while my wife slept, and thought that I slept too, what peril was possible for me to fall into.'* It was Dame Alice's daughter, Alice Alington, to whom their hopes turned late in that summer of 1534. The Alingtons' nearest neighbours at Horseheath were the Barnardiston family. Sir Thomas Barnardiston's daughter was married to Lord Audley, and his son Thomas to Mary, daughter of Sir Edmund Walsingham who, as Lieutenant of the Tower, had custody of More, and eventually supervised his execution.[132] Audley was a frequent visitor to the home of his father-in-law, at Ketton hall, to the east of the Horseheath estate. The two families were close friends. On one such visit, he had asked Sir Giles if he could come over and shoot a buck on the Horseheath estate. To the Alingtons, deeply distressed at the predicament of Alice's stepfather in the Tower, the opportunity seemed heaven sent, to ask his assistance for More. He had in February of that year interceded on More's behalf to the King, to have his name struck off an Act of Attainder. The young Alice had high hopes that after a good day's sport at Horseheath he might be willing to speak for her stepfather again. He seemed anxious to help, and asked her to come over to Sir Thomas Barnardiston's the following day, to discuss More's situation with him. She describes the visit in a letter to Margaret Roper:

> *'The Lord Chancellor had come to take a course at a buck in our park, the which*
> *was to my husbands great comfort, that it would please him to do so.*
> *Then when he had taken his pleasure, and killed his deer, he went to*
> *Sir Thomas Barnstones to bed, where I was with him the next day,*
> *at his desire, the which I could not say nay, for me thought*
> *he did bid me heartily, and most especially because I would speak*
> *with him for my father.'*[133]

Hopes rose in the Alington household that night, between the shooting party, and Alice's visit to Ketton Hall the following day, that he might intervene for More again. The Chancellor had been in an excellent humour, and anxious to hear the news of More from his stepdaughter. But when Alice spoke with Audley it was obvious that he had no intention of helping More. He made it clear that he thought it was time More came to his senses, and got himself out of his predicament by his own excellent wits. He mentioned two Aesop fables to illustrate his point, one being of the wise man who, on trying to rule fools, was in fact beaten by the foolish majority. Poor Alice was shocked by his attitude, and lack of concern, and bitterly disappointed. She concludes her letter on a sorrowful note:

'In faith the fables pleased me not a thing, nor wist I not what to say, for I was abashed by his answer. And I see no better suit than to Almighty God, for he is the comforter of all sorrows, and will not fail to send his comfort to his servants when they have most need.'[134]

Margaret Roper took Alice Alington's letter to the Tower on her next visit, for her father to read. He read it slowly through twice, and was obviously deeply moved by her efforts on his behalf. Not only was Dame Alice's daughter the only person of the family to be in a position to plead for More to the Chancellor, but it was to her that one of the most remarkable letters from the Tower was written. It was first published by Nicholas Harpsfield, from a copy of the original. It is therefore difficult to be sure how much of it was written by Margaret Roper, and how much by More himself. That it was joint effort is not doubted. It is written in the form of a dialogue, therefore Alice Alington is referred to in the third person. That two such distinguished people took such trouble over this wonderful letter, is a great tribute to Alice Alington. More speaks lovingly of his gratitude to her, and draws attention to the fine husband and household that she has, and also remembers her first husband, Thomas Elrington:

'I find my daughter Alice such as I have ever found her, and I trust ever shall, as naturally thinking of me as you that are my own. And I take her verily for mine own, too, since I have married her mother, and brought her up from childhood, as I have brought up you, in other things, and in learning, both wherein I thank God she finds some fruit, and brings her own up very virtuously and well; whereof God, I thank him, has sent her good store. Our Lord preserve them, and send her much joy of them, and my good son, her gentle husband too; and have mercy on the soul of my other good son, her first husband. I am her daily bedesman (and so write her) for them all. In this matter she has behaved like herself, wisely and like a true daughter to me, and in the end of her letter gives as good council as any man that hath wit would wish; God give me grace to follow it, and God reward her for it.'[135]

Without incriminating himself in any way, More, in this letter to Alice Alington, shows as much of his heart and faith as he ever showed to any one in these last months of his life. It should be quoted here, not only as the heart of More's belief, but also as throwing light on the fine character of Dame Alice's daughter, to whom it was written:

'I know well mine own conscience causes me to refuse the oath, so will I trust in God that according to their consciences, they have received it and sworn. But where as you think, Margaret, that there are so many more than there are on the other side, that think in this thing as I think, surely for your own comfort, that you should not be anxious, thinking that your father casts himself away like a fool, that he would hazard the loss of his substance and perhaps his body too, without any cause why he should do so for the peril of his soul, but rather put his soul in peril thereby too, this shall I say to you, Margaret, that in some of my causes

I nothing doubt at all that, though not in this realm, yet in all Christendom round about, there are well learned men still alive who are not the fewer to think as I do. Besides that you know well that it is possible that some men in this realm, too, do not think so clearly the contrary as by the oath received they have sworn to say.

Now thus far forth I say for such as are still alive. But let me go now to those that are dead, and that are, I trust, in heaven, I am sure that it is not in the fewer part of them that all the time while they were alive thought in some of the things the way that I think now. I am also of this thing sure enough, that of those holy doctors and saints who are with God in heaven long ago, as no good Christian man doubts, whose books still remain here today in men's hands, there were some who thought such things as I think now.

I say not that they all thought so, but surely such and so many as will well appear by their writing, that I pray God give me the grace that my soul may follow theirs.

And yet I show you not all that I have for myself in that sure discharge of my conscience. But for the conclusion of all this matter, as I have often told you, I take not upon me either to define or dispute in these matters, nor do I rebuke or impugn any other man's deeds, nor did I ever write or so much as speak in any company any word of reproach in anything that the Parliament has passed, nor do I meddle with the conscience of any other man, who either thinks, or says he thinks, contrary to mine.

But as concerning mine own self, for thy comfort shall I say, daughter, to you, that mine own conscience in this matter (I damn no other mans), is such as may well stand with mine own salvation. Of that, Meg, I am sure as that God is in heaven. And therefore as for all the rest, goods, land, and life both (if the chance should turn out) since this conscience is so sure for me, I verily trust in God he shall rather strengthen me to bear the loss than against this conscience swear and put my soul in peril, since all the causes I perceive move other men to the contrary, seem not such unto me as to make any change in my conscience.

And therefore my good daughter, never trouble your mind for anything that shall ever happen to me in this world. Nothing can come, but that which God wills. And I am very sure that whatsoever that may be, however bad it may appear, it shall indeed be the best.

And with this my good child, I pray you heartily, you and all your sisters, and my sons too, be comforting and servicible to your good mother, my wife. And of your good husband's minds I have no kind of doubt. Commend me to them all, and to my good daughter Alice, and to all my other friends, sisters, nieces, nephews, and allies, (relations by marriage), and unto all our servants, man, woman, and child, and all my good neighbours, and our acquaintance abroad. And I right heartily pray both you and them to serve God, and be merry and rejoice in him. And if anything happen to me that you would be loath, pray to God for me, but trouble not yourself, as I shall full heartily pray for us all that we may meet together once in heaven, where we shall be merry for ever, and never have trouble after.'[136]

When this moving and remarkable letter reached Horseheath, it made a deep impression on the family not least perhaps Dame Alice's three eldest grandsons, Thomas and John Elrington, then thirteen and twelve years old, and Richard Alington, ten. We shall hear later how John Elrington was to be branded as a *'filthy traitor'* for his defence of the principle for which More died. Dame Alice continued to plead with More to save his own life: *'And how long, my Alice, shall I be able to enjoy this life,'* he asks her. *'A full twenty years,'* she replied, *'if God so wills. Do you wish me then to change eternity for twenty years?'*

'Nay good wife, you do not bargain very skillfully. If you had said some thousand of years, you would have said something, but what would that be in comparison with eternity?'

A Deep Rooted Scruple

'My husband is suffering from a long continued and deep rooted scruple, as passeth his power to avoid or put aside'[137]
LADY ALICE MORE IN A PETITION TO THE KING

FROM THE THIRD OF NOVEMBER, when the new sitting of Parliament brought in an Act of Attainder against More and Fisher, More's life in the Tower changed. Most of the privileges he had enjoyed through the summer were withdrawn. The most tragic for him were the loss of frequent visits from the family, and the joy of going to daily Mass. His supply of books was also curtailed.

Until now the King had allowed Dame Alice to keep the rents and other income from her husband's property. Under the new charge of treason his property would be forfeit to the King. At the time of his imprisonment, More owed the King a large sum of money. The burden of repaying this fell on his son John. There is no suggestion that the Ropers, Daunceys and Herons were penalised in any way at this stage. It is certain that by January 1535, Dame Alice was paying for the keep of More and his servant, in the Tower, out of her own finances. Little or no help seemed to come from More's sons-in-law. This may have been due to their fear of repercussions on their own families, or they knew that Alice could well afford to pay; or perhaps it is another example of lack of sensitivity on their part. The exaggerated reports of Dame Alice's poverty at this time may, of course, have been a deliberate policy worked out by More and his wife. Under an Act of Attainder the Crown could not confiscate what they could not find. There are several indications in More's last few letters from the Tower, that this was in fact the situation.

Dame Alice was not only deeply worried by the peril her husband was in, and her own threatened financial difficulties, but was also distressed at his rapidly declining health, caused by the deterioration in his prison conditions. In the accounts of the Tower of London for 1537, the accountant notes that Dame Alice still owed that inhospitable establishment £9, outstanding for her husband's keep and that of his servant.[138] It would seem that as a protest at his poor lodging, and also to keep up the pretence of dire poverty, Dame Alice had refused to pay for his last three months in the Tower.

She wrote a letter to the King, putting to him More's plight, her own, and that of his son John:

> *'Thus, except your merciful favour be shown your said poor bedeswoman, his wife, which brought fair substance to him,* (one of the few references to her own personal wealth), *which is all spent in your Grace's service, is likely to be utterly undone, and his poor son, one of your humble suppliants, standing charged and bound for great sums of money due by the said Sir Thomas to your Grace, standeth in danger to be cast away and undone in this world also. But over all this the said Sir Thomas himself is likely to be in his age and continual sickness, for lack of comfort and good keeping, to be shortly destroyed, to the woeful heaviness and deadly discomfort of all your said suppliants.'*[139]

Needless to say the letter went unanswered. It probably only got as far as the desk of Master Secretary Cromwell, and was not seen by the King at all.

This first letter of appeal by Dame Alice was written mainly out of concern for her husband's health during the winter cold, that was making his symptoms of ague and acute cramp, well nigh intolerable (especially at night).

Early in the new year of 1535, with the passing of the new Act of Supremacy, three of More's manors were taken from him and given to Sir Henry Norris, of Rycote, near Thame, Oxfordshire. They were Ducklington, Fringford, in Oxfordshire, and Barley Park in Hertfordshire, near Royston. Norris was a great favourite of Anne Boleyn, and because of his friendship with her, (probably quite innocent), he enjoyed More's property for less than a year before he found himself in the appalling position of being condemned as a traitor for an affair with the Queen, and was himself executed in 1536. A similar fate awaited the other recipient of More's confiscated property, the Queen's brother, George Boleyn, Lord Rochford. He had acquired the More's manor of South, between Tunbridge Wells and Tonbridge, in Kent.[140] Accused and convicted of incest with his sister, the Queen, he also went to the scaffold with his friend Norris.

In a letter to Margaret Roper, More mentions the possibility of searches being made in all their houses, and there is a broad hint here that the wily Dame Alice had already spirited away all the valuable property, before the King's men arrived. She would have had a wide choice of establishments where they might have been concealed; the manors of Denecourt and Willesdon, for example, were still in the possession of her daughter, as well as Horseheath Hall, and her own property at Hitchin. More wrote:

> 'Some folks ween that I was not so poor as it appeared in the search,
> and that it may therefore happen again soon, oftener than once,
> some new sudden searches may happen to be made in every house of ours,
> as narrowly as is possible. Which thing if ever it should so happen, can
> make but game to us who know the truth of my poverty, but if they find out my
> wife's gay girdle, and her golden beads. Howbeit, I verily believe in good faith,
> that the King's Grace of his benign pity, will take nothing from her.'[141]

It would have been a bold officer who dared to rob Dame Alice of such cherished possessions! There is a warning in this letter to Dame Alice that he expects further visits of the King's officers, and no doubt she took the necessary evasive action. Alice's kinship with the King also, as More knew, stood her in good stead where her own personal possessions were concerned.

Wonderful as More's letters to his daughter are, for their deep spirituality and learning, it is sad that none of the many letters he must have written to his wife during the fifteen months of his imprisonment in the Tower have survived, or if they have, they have not been discovered. Dame Alice would have looked upon her husband's correspondence to her as private, and as much of it was involved in household affairs, and how to cope with the threat and likelihood of all her husband's possessions and property being confiscated, she may well have destroyed his letters as a safety precaution.

After the loss of the manor at South, Dame Alice wrote directly to Cromwell. The letter is quoted in full as it shows that other correspondence must have taken place between Alice and the King, which is lost. To mention the health of one of her servants is an indication that the affairs of the household had been discussed between them prior to this letter.

> 'Right Honorable, and my especyall gud Maister Secretary, in my most
> humble wyse I recommend me unto your good Mastership, knowledging
> myself to be most deeply boundyn to your good Maistership for your
> manifold Gudness and loving favour, both before this time, and yet dayly,
> now also shewed towards my poure husband and me. I pray Almighty
> God continew your Gudness so Styll, for thereupon hangith the greatest

*Part of my poure husband's comfort and myne. The cause of my writing
at this tyme, is to certify your especiall gud Maistership of my great and
extreem necessyte which on, and besides the charge of myne own House,
do pay weekly 15 shillings for the board-wages of my poure husband, and
his servant; for the maintaining whereof I have been compelled of very
necessity, to sell part of myne own Apparell, for lack of other substance
to make money of. Whereof my most humble petition and Sewte to your
Maistership at this time, is to desyre your Maistership's favourable Advise
and Counsell, whether I may be so bold to attend upon the King's most
gracyouse Highness. I trust there is no doubt in the cause of my
Impediment: for the young man, being a ploughman, had been dyseased
with the aggue by the space of three years before that he departed, and no
other person deseased in the house since that time: wherefore I humbly
beseach your especial gud Maistership, for the love of God to consider the
Premisses, and thereupon of your most abundant gudness to shew your
most favourable help in the comforting of my poor husband and me, in
this our great heaviness, extreem age, and necessity. And thus we, and
all ours, shall dayly during our lives, pray to God for the prosperous
Success of your ryght honourable Dygnyty. By your poure contynuall
oratrice, Dame Alice More.'*[142]

There is no record that she received a reply.

From this letter, it is apparent that Alice had been to court herself, to
see the King, and that a visit was not unusual. The fact that a ploughman's
illness seems to have been the reason for her not seeing him on this
occasion was the excuse that was given for refusing to see her.

More was reconciled to the loss of his home, but as his imprisonment
continued, with only rare visits from his family, and his health broke
down, he most touchingly complains in one of his last letters to Margaret,
of how much he misses talking to his wife and friends:

*'Not since I came here did I ever long to set foot in my own house for
any desire of, or pleasure in my house, but gladly would I sometimes talk
with my friends, and especially my wife, and you that do pertain to my
charge.'*[143]

He then goes on to imply that, like all mixed families, they had not
always lived peacefully together. With such strong personalities as Dame
Alice and William Roper living in close contact with each other it was

Thomas Cromwell / The Kylin Archive.

hardly surprising. More must often have had to restore harmony between them. He continues:

> 'Since God disposes otherwise, I commit all wholly to his goodness, and take daily comfort in that I perceive that you live together so charitably and quietly; I beseech our Lord to continue it.'[144]

Margaret pays a generous tribute to her stepmother in her letter to More on hearing how his liberty was now curtailed:

> 'Father, what moved them to shut you up again, we can nothing hear, but surely I conjecture that when they considered that you were of so temperate a mind, that you were content to abide there all your life with such liberty, they thought it were impossible to incline you to their will except it were by restraining you from the Church, and the company of my good mother, your wife, and us children and bedesfolk.'[145]

Margaret knew of the great delight her father always took in her stepmother's company, and how she always managed to keep him in good heart during the long months of imprisonment. More answers her by referring to the death penalty that the new Act of Supremacy carried:

> 'Now have I heard that some say that the obstinate manner of mine in still refusing the oath, shall peradventure force the King's Grace to make a further law for me. I cannot let (hinder) such a law to be made. But I am very sure that if I died by such a law, I should die for that point, innocent before God.'[146]

Like a doctor who can diagnose his own mortal illness, More, with his knowledge of the law, and of his king, was fully aware of his certain death if the new law was enforced.

His feelings for his master, the King, were put down in a stanza that he added to *Verses on Fortune*, written thirty years before:

> 'Eye flattering Fortune, look thou never so fair,
> Nor never so pleasantly begin to smile,
> As though thou wouldst my ruin all repair;
> During my life thou shalt not me begile.
> Trust shall I god to enter awhile
> His haven of Heaven, sure and uniform;
> Ever after thy calm, look I for a storm.' [147]

A Matter of Conscience

'Give my thy Grace, good Lord . . . to think my most enemies my best friends . . .'

THOMAS MORE, WRITTEN IN THE MARGIN OF HIS PRAYER BOOK,
IN THE TOWER

ALTHOUGH THE ACT of Supremacy, and the Acts of Attainder against More and Fisher, went through Parliament on 3 November 1534, the first interrogations did not take place until the 30 April. The second occurred on 4 May, after More and his daughter Margaret had watched from the window of More's room the Carthusian monks being drawn on hurdles out of the courtyard, on their terrible road to Tyburn, which was situated where Marble Arch is today. In More's poor state of health, they would both have known that if he was condemned to a similar fate, he would probably never survive the journey. Margaret may have been allowed to see him that day in the hope that she could make him change his mind.

He was interrogated for the third time on 3 June, and between this and his final interrogation on 14 June, More was visited by Richard Rich, the Solicitor General. This clever young lawyer was born in the parish of St Stephen's Walbrook, and Dame Alice and her husband had known him in the old days, when they lived at The Barge in Bucklersbury. It is important to realise that not only had the Mores known Richard Rich for a long time, but that his family had close connections with Dame Alice's through the Harpurs and the Shaas. His grandfather, Thomas Rich, who appears to have been, unlike his grandson, a man of integrity, was a prominent member of the Mercers Company and a colleague of Dame Alice's first husband, John Middleton.[148] Thomas Rich was also a friend of her father, Sir Richard Harpur, and cousin of Sir John Shaa, who bought Markhall from the Ardern family.[149] More himself had been involved with the Shaa family since 1525, when Sir John's son Edmund Shaa went insane, and More was put in charge of his affairs for him, including the Markhall estate.[150] To have such a man as Richard Rich paying More a visit in the Tower, with the intention of trapping him into a treasonable confession, was bad enough for Dame Alice, but at least both she and her husband knew the type of man he was, and More would have been well on his guard against him. But apart from the two servants, the man who accompanied Rich was an even closer connection of Dame Alice, Richard Southwell, who was the nephew and heir of her cousin by marriage, Robert Southwell.[151]

As the excuse for this visit was ostensibly to pack up More's books, Southwell may, due to his connection with Dame Alice, have been asked by her to collect them and bring them back to Chelsea, rather than let them fall into someone else's hands. But it has been mentioned before that Sir Peter Ardern had left a remarkable collection of books, some of which were mentioned specifically in his will to come to Sir John Skreene, Elizabeth Ardern's first husband. She inherited his estate, and it is quite likely that she passed on this collection of law books to her son-in-law, Thomas More, on his marriage to Alice.[152]

Whatever the reason for Southwell being with Rich, and packing up More's books, it is to his great credit that he refused to be involved in the perjury that Rich committed at More's trial. When called as a witness, he said, in his deposition that *'He was appointed only to look into the conveyance of his books, and gave no ear to the conversation'.* It was a tragedy for Dame Alice that the two men who went to More's cell on that fatal day, when Rich trumped up the evidence against More that was to result in his death, should have been connected with her family. More's indictment was based on Richard Rich's perjured evidence of what More had said in this conversation in the Tower, which stated that More spoke treasonably against the Act. A document in the Public Record office, found recently, much damaged by damp and rats, gives enough evidence to show that this was the actual conversation that More had with Rich, where Rich warns him of the danger he is in because he has not answered the questions as he should have done. The indictment, read out at the trial was much altered from the original.[153]

At his trial More delivers one of the most scathing accounts of Rich's characters:

> *'You know that I have been acquainted with your manner of life and*
> *conversation for a long time, for we dwelt together in one parish, where, as you*
> *yourself can well tell, (I am sorry you compel me to speak), you were always*
> *esteemed very light of your tongue, a great dicer and gamester,*
> *and not of any commendable fame there, or at your house at the Temple, where*
> *hath been your bringing up.'*[154]

Baron Richard Rich / reproduced by gracious permission of Her Majesty the Queen.

More and his wife had entertained this unscrupulous young man too often, and knew him only too well for More to think of revealing to him any of his deep feelings. Dame Alice's long acquaintance with him prepared her and the rest of the family for the perjured evidence that he was to produce against her husband at his trial, on 1 July. Appalled as they must have been when they realized that he was to be the chief witness against More, the behaviour of this man whom they had befriended cannot have come as a surprise, particularly to such a realist as Dame Alice.

Richard Rich, this political Vicar of Bray, who turned his coat to suit each new reign, owed his success, and eventual position as Lord Chancellor, to his despicable habit of climbing to fame on the backs of his colleagues and friends, and then destroying them. His personal racking of Anne Askew in the Tower, in 1544, was considered, by J. A. Froude, to be *'the darkest page in the history of any statesman.'* The summing up of his character in the *D.N.B.* gives a very clear idea of the type of man who, as a rising lawyer, was only too glad to accept the hospitality of More and his wife and yet had no scruples in betraying him:

> *'He was a time server of the least admirable type, he was always found on the winning side, and he had a hand in the ruin of most of the prominent men of his time, not a few of whom had been his friends and benefactors Wolsey, More, Fisher, Cromwell, Wriothesley, Lord Seymour of Sudeley,* (Catherine Parr's fourth husband), *Somerset and Northumberland. His readiness to serve the basest ends of tyranny and power, justifies his description as one of the most ominous names in the history of the age.'*[155]

More's own words, when he has read Rich's evidence, ring down the centuries:

> *'In good faith, Master Rich, I am sorrier for your perjury than I am for mine own peril. And you should understand that neither I, nor any man else to my knowledge, ever took you to be a man of such credit as in any matter of importance I, or any other, would at any time vouch safe to communicate with you. Can it therefore seem likely, to your honourable lordships that I would in so weighty a case, so unadvisedly overshoot myself as to trust Master Rich, (a man of men always reputed for one of so little trust, as your lordships have heard), so far above my Sovereign, the king, or any of his noble councillors, that I would unto him utter the secrets of my conscience touching the King's Supremacy, the special point, and only mark at my hands so sought for, a thing which I never did, nor never would, after the statute therefor made, reveal either to the King's highness himself, or to any of his honourable councillors, as it is not unknown to your honours, at sundry times sent from his Grace's own*

person to the Tower to me for none other purpose? Can this, in your
judgements, my lords, seem likely to be true?'[156]

As far as we know, none of the family were present at More's trial in Westminster Hall, but hearing how her husband spoke out against the perjury of the young man who had taken her hospitality must have pleased Dame Alice. We may be sure, too, that Lord Audley, as Chairman of the Court, was ill at ease. He found himself in the unenviable position of sitting in judgement on a former Lord Chancellor, and a man who was a better lawyer than himself; nor can he have forgotten the hospitality of Dame Alice's daughter and her husband, Giles Alington, nor that daughter's pleas for her stepfather.

As the trial progresses, Audley appears to make several elementary blunders in the conducting of it. Firstly, as Southwell and the other two men in More's cell with them at the time, Master Palmer, and Master Derleght, all refused to corroborate Rich's evidence, Audley should not have allowed the jury to pass judgement on the evidence of one man alone. Secondly, he should not have proceeded to pass judgement before the prisoner in the dock had a chance to speak. More had to remind him of his blunder, whereupon Audley allowed him to address the court.

A newsletter which appeared in Paris two weeks after More's execution gives the earliest account of the trial. It states that in his address to the Court, More at last spoke out on his refusal to take the oath. The travesty of justice that was meted out to him made it pointless to hold his peace any longer. His opening statement must have made a great impression on his hearers:

> *'Seeing that I see that ye are determined to condemn me, (God knoweth how) I*
> *will now, in discharge of my conscience speak my mind plainly and freely*
> *touching my Indictment, and your Statute withal. As for as much as this*
> *Indictment is grounded upon an Act of Parliament directly repugnant to the*
> *laws of God, and His Holy Church, the supreme government of which,*
> *or any part thereof, may no temporal prince presume by law to*
> *take upon him, as rightfully belonging to the See of Rome.'*

By uttering such words in such a place, More was a dead man. Later in his speech, he continued:

> *'Such an action was contrary to the sacred Oath which the King's highness*
> *himself, and every other Christian Prince, always, with great solemnity,*
> *received at their Coronation; alleging, moreover that no more might*
> *this realm of England refuse obedience to the See of Rome than might*
> *the child refuse obedience to his natural father.'*

Here the Duke of Norfolk interrupted him:

'We now plainly see that ye are maliciously bent,' to which More replied:
'Nay, nay, very and pure necessity for the discharge of my conscience forceth
me to speak so much. Wherein I call and appeal to God, whose only sight
pierceth into the very depth of a man's heart, to be my witness.
Howbeit it is not for this Supremacy so much that ye seek my blood,
as for that I would not condescend to the marriage.'

The Lord Chancellor hesitated. He turned to the Lord Chief Justice Lord
FitzJames for advice as to whether the Indictment was good law or not. It would
appear that Lord Audley, far too late in the day, was making a last minute
attempt to save More's life. Lord FitzJames replied *'My Lords all, by Saint Julien*
(his favourite oath), *I must needs confess that if the Act of Parliament be not unlawful,*
then is not the Indictment in my conscience insufficient.' An ambiguous reply that cost
More his life. Lord Audley then condemned More to death at Tyburn, by
hanging, drawing and quartering.

Owing to the tide, More was not taken back to the Tower through the
Traitors Gate, but was taken by barge to the Old Swan Steps. The family had
been waiting for the verdict outside Westminster Hall, and they rushed to the
steps to take their final farewell of him. Dame Alice, as his wife, would have
been allowed a last visit to him in his cell. His friend, Sir William Kingston,
Constable of the Tower, accompanied him as far as the steps, and then made a
sad farewell. Through his bitter tears he found that instead of being able to
comfort More, he received solace from him. He described the scene to Roper:

'In good faith I was ashamed of myself, that at departing from your father, I
found my heart so feeble, and his so strong, that he was fain to comfort me,
which should have rather comforted him.'[157]

Margaret Roper, John More, his wife Anne, and Margaret Clement knelt at
the steps, as he got out of his barge, where he gave each his blessing, Margaret
Roper rushing back to him for a second, final embrace, before the guard took
him through the gate, back to his cell.

Although there is no mention directly in any of the biographies of More that
Dame Alice visited him after his conviction, and before his execution, there are
several good reasons for supposing that she did. Firstly, it was the usual practice
that a condemned man would be allowed to see his wife, and Dame Alice would

certainly have insisted on her rights over this. Secondly, in his last letter from the Tower, written in haste and unfinished, to Margaret Roper, he mentions all the family, except his wife, by name, even the grandchildren and servants. If he was seeing his wife, there would be no need to mention her; she may have actually carried the letter from the Tower to Margaret herself. In this letter he is clearly right up to date with the current news of the family and servants at Chelsea, in particular about some domestic trouble involving a servant. It was his wife who always kept him informed about these household matters, and it is unlikely that anyone else would have been allowed access to him but his wife, who could have given him such intimate news. The most likely explanation was that Dame Alice was making her last visit to him when he wrote it, and her having to leave before the letter was finished would account for its abrupt end:

'Our Lord bless you, good daughter, and your good husband, and your little boy, and all yours, and all my children, and all my godchildren and all our friends. Recommend me, when you may to my good daughter Cecily, who I beseech our Lord comfort. And I send her my blessing and to all her children, and pray her to pray for me. I send her a handkerchief, and God comfort my good son her husband. My good daughter Dauncey hath the parchment picture that you delivered me from Lady Conyers, her name is on the back side.

I liked especially well Dorothy Colley. I pray you be good to her. I should like to know if this be she that you wrote me of. If not yet I pray you be good to the other as you may in her affliction, and to my good daughter, Joan Aleyn. Give her I pray you, some kind answer, for she sued hither to me this day. I send now unto my good daughter Clement, her algorism stone. I send her and my good son her husband and all hers, God's blessing and mine. I pray you at a time convenient recommend me to my good son, John More. I liked well his natural fashion. Our Lord bless him, and his good wife, my loving daughter, to whom I pray him be good, as he hath great cause, and if the land of mine come into his hands, he break not my will concerning his sister Dauncey. And our lord bless Thomas and Austin and all that they shall have.'[158]

Comforter of all sorrows

'I see no better suit than to Almighty God, for he is the comforter of all sorrows. . .'
LADY ALICE ALINGTON

'O God, the Resurrection and the Life of them that put their trust in Thee, who art always to be praised as well in the Dead as in the Living, we yield Thee thanks for Thomas Pope Knight, our Founder, and the Lady Elizabeth, his wife, deceased, and for all other our Benefactors, by whose Liberality we are here brought up in Godliness and Learning.'[159]

THE PRESIDENT OF TRINITY COLLEGE, OXFORD has been giving thanks for the Founder, Sir Thomas Pope, who was Sir Thomas and Lady More's *'singular good friend'*. Later sitting quietly in the sun of the President's garden, flanked by the ancient walls of the original Durham College, it is good to remember that not all the young men that the Mores befriended were of the quality of Richard Rich. Master Thomas Pope was much beloved by them both, and a frequent visitor to their home, and was the last friend More saw before he died.

He was born in 1507, and by 1535 was a member of Lord Audley's household, where he was living at the time of More's death. Since 1534 he had been Warden of the Royal Mint, which was situated in the Tower of London. As More's *'singular good friend'* he would have been a frequent visitor to him during his imprisonment. When the time for More's execution was fixed, it was a kindly gesture of Audley's or perhaps the King's, to send one of More's great friends, a young man of twenty-eight to break the news to him.

In the early morning of 6 July, Master Pope arrived at More's cell. His conversation with More, later recounted to his friend William Roper, is deeply moving. Having had the news broken to him, More replies:

'Master Pope for your good tidings I most heartily thank you. I have always been much bounden to the King's Highness for the benefits and honours that he

*Thomas Pope, the great friend of Lady Alice and Sir Thomas /
from the Author's collection.*

hath still from time to time most bountifully heaped upon me;
and yet more bound am I to his Grace for putting me into this place,
where I have had convenient time and space to have rememberence of mine end.
And so help me God most of all, Master Pope, and I am bound to his
Highness that it pleaseth him so shortly to rid me out of the miseries of
this world. And therefore I will pray earnestly for his Grace, both here
and in the next world.'

Pope knew More's bantering way of talking well, and was amazed that even in this extremity, he never lost his light touch. But he had more bad news to break. More was renowned as a fine orator, and it was expected that his speech from the scaffold would be the finest of his life. Because of the danger of its effect on the onlookers, the King was determined that it should not be made. *'The King's pleasure,'* the unhappy Pope went on, *'is that at your execution you will not use many words.'* More looked downcast at this news and the bantering tones are dropped for the reply:

'Master Pope, you do me well to give me a warning of his Grace's pleasure. For
otherwise I was purposed at that time somewhat to have spoken,
but of no matter wherewith his Grace, or any other should have cause
to be offended. Nevertheless, whatsoever I had intended I am readily
obedient to conform myself to his Grace's commandments.'

That his wife would be at his burial would have been taken for granted, so he goes on to beg Pope to ask the King if his daughter Margaret can also be there. Pope here has some comfort for him. *'The King is content,'* he replied, *'that your wife, children and other of your friends shall have liberty to be present thereat.'*

'O how much beholden then, am I to his Grace,' replies More, *'that unto my poor burial vouchsafeth to have so gracious consideration. This man might have lived longer if it had pleased the King.'*

The return of More's humour was too much for his broken-hearted friend, and Master Pope burst into tears. More comforted him, as he had comforted Sir William Kingston a few days earlier. *'Quiet yourself, Master Pope, and be not discomforted; for I trust that we shall one day in heaven see each other full merrily, where we shall be sure to live and love together, in joyful bliss eternally.'*[160]

More's sentence had been changed from the brutal death by hanging, drawing and quartering usually meted out to commoners, to the more humane one of beheading. This may have been a gesture of mercy by the King to his old friend. There was also the danger of the crowd being outraged at seeing a beloved Lord Chancellor being dragged on a hurdle to Tyburn, a journey that in his poor state of health he would have been unlikely to survive.

After the departure of Thomas Pope he had only a few short hours to prepare for his execution. Sir Edward Walsingham, Lieutenant of the Tower, was with him, and was surprised to see him dressing himself in a fine robe of camlet, a very expensive material of silk and wool, a present from his old and faithful friend, Bonvisi. Usually so careless about dress, he may have promised Dame Alice on her last visit that he should wear the gown for her sake, and for the sake of their great mutual friend. His determination to wear it must have had more reason behind it than making a present of it to the executioner, whose perquisite it would become. Sadly, after much argument, he bowed to Walsingham's wishes. After all, Walsingham said, the executioner was only a javel (a low fellow and a rascal). *'What, Master Lieutenant, shall I count him a javel that shall do me this day such a singular benefit? Nay, I assure you, were it cloth of gold, I would account it well bestowed on him, as Saint Cyprian did who gave his executioner thirty pieces of gold.'*[161] Walsingham and More had both been at the Field of the Cloth of Gold, and would remember the glittering scene.

Bearing in mind Master Pope's warning that he was not to make a long speech on the scaffold, he was now faced with the kind of challenge that he would normally have enjoyed, to pack all he had wished to say into the few brief words allowed him. The only member of the Chelsea household to be at his execution was the gallant Margaret Clement, who heard his last words. The King had forbidden the rest of the family to be there. The unknown reporter of the *Paris News Letter* described the last scene:

'He spoke little before his execution. Only he asked the bystanders to pray for him, and he would pray for them elsewhere. He then begged them to pray for the King, that it might please God to give him good council, protesting that he died the King's good servant but God's first.'[162]

Professor Chambers states that he considers More's last words the haughtiest ever spoken from the scaffold.[163] Nicholas Harpsfield said *'He was the first layman in England that died a martyr for the defence and preservation of the Catholic Church, and that is his special peerless prerogative.'*[164]

So ended this remarkable marriage of Thomas and Alice, that had lasted for twenty-four years. It had been full of love, laughter, high hopes, bitter disappointments, some anger, mis-understanding and tears. Through it all Dame Alice remained steadfast and loyal to the end. It is difficult to imagine the grief of such an indomitable lady for the tragic, and to her unnecessary death of such a husband. Stapleton, writing twenty years after the execution, mentions that Roper's wife, Margaret and her maid, and Margaret Clements were at

More's burial in St Peter's ad Vincula, in the precincts of the Tower, but he does not mention Dame Alice as being one of the party.[165] This omission naturally puts her presence there out of the reader's mind. But we know from Master Pope's conversation with More, that Dame Alice had permission to attend her husband's funeral, and it can surely be assumed that she made one of the sorrowful party that laid his headless body to rest in a grave, not 400 yards from where the body of her former husband John Middleton lay, in St Katherine Coleman.

In a file on the Middleton family in the Society of Genealogists is a tattered notebook. The following words, roughly pencilled in, might have been written by Dame Alice herself as she left the grave of her second husband in St Peter ad Vincula. They are in fact Macaulay's:

> 'There is no sadder spot on earth than this little cemetery. Death is their association, not as in Westminster Abbey and St Paul's with genius, virtue, with public veneration and imperishable renown, not as in our humblest Churches and churchyards, with everything that is most endearing in social and domestic charities; but with whatever is darkest in human nature and in human destiny; with the savage triumph of implacable enemies, with the inconstancy, the ingratitude, the cowardice of friends, with all the miseries of fallen greatness and of blighted fame.'[166]

Widow of a Traitor

*'Give me thy grace, good lord,
To be content to be solitary'*

THE GREAT HOUSE at Chelsea had been empty of her husband's presence for so long, over fifteen months, that Dame Alice, apart from the deep grief at his death, continued her former life there for some time, struggling with litigation of various kinds. Although the Act of Attainder against More had been passed by Parliament, yet owing to some technical defect, and perhaps delaying tactics on the part of Lord Audley, and even the King himself, the Royal assent was not given to it until two years later, in 1536. That Alice would ultimately have to give the house up was, of course, inevitable, but during the breathing space between More's death and the taking over of the custody of the house by Sir William Paulet, she had time to arrange some of her affairs. According to the *Patent Roll 23 Henry VIII, 1536,* Sir William was given the custody, rule and governance of the lands that had belonged to Sir Thomas More. The King wanted the rents paid into the hands of *'Thomas, our chamberlain',* for the time being. This would imply that Paulet did not come into possession of the estate, but was its steward and administrator. Thus Dame Alice may well have been in residence there until 1544.

As mentioned before, the more valuable possessions had been moved out of the Court's jurisdiction. Although Cresacre More complained, when he came to write his great grandfather's life, that the King's men had destroyed all the family papers, it seems more likely that Dame Alice forestalled them by doing it herself. The Ropers had been fortunate enough to have had the lease of the house where they lived transferred to them completely in 1534, so it was not attainted with More's other property. More's attempts to transfer the Great House and his other manors to trustees were made too late for them to be completed. The family had their houses searched but nothing of a seditious nature was discovered. In 1538 Margaret Roper and Margaret Clement were taken into custody for a short time and questioned, but released.

To raise some capital from the estates before the Act of Attainder was ratified, Dame Alice endeavoured to dispose of some land and farm stock to a purchaser, John Lane, who was a speculator in property. The manor of Sutton Court had been acquired by More from its previous owner, a diplomat friend, Richard Pace, who died insane in 1536. Pace's delightful description of More in his *De Fructu qui ex Doctrina Percipitur* is well known: '*He is too brilliant for his own good, a great graceist, superbly eloquent in Latin and English, a laughing philosopher, who arouses the envy of men.*'

Sutton Court was a valuable asset, and the oldest of the two manors in Chiswick. It lay between the river and Turnham Green, with some 320 acres. In Cromwellian times it became the home of Oliver Cromwell's daughter, Mary, Countess of Falconberg. The manor was a very prosperous one, lying adjacent to the ferry, which was the first crossing of the Thames above London Bridge.[167] John Lane had bought several properties from the King, and feeling that he might take advantage of Dame Alice's doubtful title to the property, because of the Act of Attainder, refused to pay her for it. As can be imagined the shrewd Dame Alice, in spite of her recent bereavement, was not a little angered by this. In fact she was in a very delicate legal position, as it was only the delay in the assent to the Attainder that had prevented this property passing to the King. John Lane had his own grounds for not paying Dame Alice for the property; to do so might bring the Royal wrath down on his head, by depriving the King of money that was due to him.

On the advice of her son-in-law, Sir Giles Alington, in 1536 Dame Alice proceeded with a Bill of Complaint in Chancery against Lane, stating that she was only selling what she had a right to sell. Lane found himself in a cleft stick. On the one hand Dame Alice was taking him to court for not paying her what was due to her, and on the other was his fear of what would happen to himself, by incurring the King's anger if he did. The bill was drafted for her by Sir Giles, and commenced as follows:

'To the Right Honourable Sir Thomas Audley, Knight, Lord Chancellor of England; humbley sheweth and complaineth to your good lordship your daily orator and besceecher, Dame Alice More, in the XXVIIth year of the reign of Our Soverign Lord, King Henry VIII That now she did bargain and sale unto one, John Lane, gentleman, 350 old sheep and 136 lambs for the sum of £36 and 28 pence of the lawful money of England . . . Further

The Execution of Thomas More by Antoine Caron, circa 1590 /
by kind permission of The Chateau de Blois.

more the said defendant in the said XXVIIth year of the reign of our Sovereign Lord, King Henry VIII in consideration and for that your said oratrice should grant all her interest and goodwill unto the said defendant in a farm in the town of Chiswick in the County of Middlesex called Sutton Court, the said defendant did promise to pay £10 of the lawful money of England to be paid into your said oratrice or her assignes at the Feast of Saint Michael Archangel and the Annuciation of Our Lady, by equal even portions during the natural life of your said oratrice.'[168]

It is interesting to note that the yearly value of the Chelsea house at that time had been put at £16.

Sir Giles was able to stop the case coming into Court by persuading Lane to pay Dame Alice half what he owed her. On the public record of her Bill, Alington's mark appears at the end to indicate that the case was closed. Reprehensible though the behaviour of John Lane was over this, he was a business man, no friend of the family, and a well-known speculator. That William Roper, however, should also attempt to deprive Dame Alice of some of her income is almost incomprehensible. Dr Hitchcock, in a note in the Early English Text Society's edition of Roper's *Life of More*, clearly states the position against him:

'We should like to think that the good fortune that the Ropers had had in owning their house in Chelsea, and therefore outside the danger of having it confiscated, would have made Roper particularly careful of any claim on More's possessions by his other children and widow, but the researches of Professor C. J. Sisson have revealed great strife between him and Dame Alice.'[169]

From the time he had inherited his father's property, Well Hall, in Eltham in 1524, and property at St Dunstan's, Canterbury, Roper had been a gentleman of means. This attempt to deprive a widow, who had already lost so much of some of her livelihood, was behaviour that his late father-in-law would have found deeply shocking. The affair arose over lands in Battersea that had been granted to More by the Abbot of Westminster in 1529. After More's execution, Henry VIII allowed Dame Alice to remain in possession of them for eight years, taking the lease up to 1543. Knowing Alice's claim to the land, Roper applied for a lease of it himself, in 1541. Such tactless effrontery to any widow would rightly be condemned as heartless and unjust. Dame Alice, as we would expect, in spite of her age, reacted strongly against it.

As always, her faithful son-in-law, Sir Giles Alington, sprang to her defence, and brought a writ against Roper for compensation for the loss of the lease.[170] He was able to arbitrate satisfactorily on her behalf, and Roper had to pay her what was her due. More would have been greatly saddened by the whole affair, and one wonders why his daughter Margaret did not use her influence to prevent her husband taking such a very uncharitable stand against her stepmother. Roper got little joy out of this property so shabbily acquired and litigation over it continued, this time with one Henry Royden, until as late as 1561. A servant who was called as a witness made the comment on Dame Alice's case against Roper: *'I heard Dame Alice many times talk thereof, and was very angry when so ere she chanced to speak of the same, until she and Master Roper were agreed again.'*[171]

All one can say about the case is that Royden's love of a legal battle must have been as great as Roper's. The contest swayed to and fro, Roper succeeded in driving out Royden, or Royden, Roper, according to which monarch was on the throne. During the reign of Edward VI a rival lease was made out to a man called Philpot, who conveyed it back to Royden. In the reign of Mary I, the Catholic claim was paramount, and in 1553 the lease was made out to Roper. Under the protestant Elizabeth, Royden forcibly entered again and drove out Roper. Dame Alice, while she was alive, must have enjoyed the proceedings! Finally in 1561, Roper descended on the place at midnight and drove out Royden, and the case came into Court.[172] This long-drawn-out fight does little credit to either party. Friction that Roper caused over his father's will suggests that he could be a difficult man to have dealings with, as Dame Alice and her late husband had discovered earlier. With this litigation with Dame Alice in mind when Roper drafted the life of his father-in-law, it is not surprising that he did her less than justice in it.

There is an interesting entry in the *Letters and Papers of Henry VIII*, on some of More's attainted lands, indicating that Dame Alice and her stepmother-in-law, Lady Alice, the widow of Sir John More, owned certain lands jointly. It also indicates that as late as 1541 these lands were still in the hands of the two women. It would imply that the King was dealing lightly with them and that the attainder up to that date had not been fully enforced. The entry reads:

> *'Lands late of Sir Thomas More, lately attainted . . . Ann (sic) Lady More,*
> *widow of Sir Thomas for lands etc in Chelsea, Middlesex.*
> *Thomas Bearne, collector of rents in Chelsea. Alice, relict of Sir John More,*
> *father of the said Sir Thomas, for a messuage called Gobions in North Mimms,*
> *Herts. The said Alice and Ann for four tenements in the parish of St Peter's,*
> *Hatfield, and for a barn, etc in Chelmsford, Essex.*

Forfeited Lands in the office of John Ashton, auditor. Arrearages due in minister's accounts, and account of particular receivers, anno 32 Henry VIII.' [173]

There is a record of more dealings in land in the Feet of Fines for Hertfordshire, this time some of Dame Alice's property in Hitchin being involved:

'Between Richard Lacy, clerk, plaintiff, and Alice More, widow, Sir Giles Alington, Knight, and Alice his wife, deforciants as to six messuage, 70 acres of land, six acres of pasture in Hitchin, Ipolletts and Offley which deforciants quit claim and warrant against themselves and the heirs of Alice the wife to plaintiff, receiving £240. ' [174]

This was a considerable sum of money for those times; the property was probably part of John Middleton's estate, in trust for Alice Alington.'

The Crown, it would appear, dealt more kindly with her than her stepson-in-law did, as in 1537 an annuity of £20 a year was granted to her, to date from the previous Michaelmas. Lady Alice's name appears regularly, year by year, in the Tellers Rolls of the exchequer, until 1547, the year of Henry VIII's death, when her name suddenly disappears. The Rolls of the first few years of Edward VI's reign seem to be coping with arrears, which may be why her pension does not appear. She is mentioned in other documents during the first few years of Edward's reign, but he was obviously not as punctilious as Henry VIII over Lady Alice's welfare. [175]

In 1539 the fear in which the whole family lived was turned into stark reality when Giles Heron, husband of Cecily, and Dame Alice's right hand man of affairs at the Great House, was arrested on a trumped-up charge of High Treason. This was a terrible blow, not only for his wife and three children, but for Alice, who had depended on him for so much. Son and heir of Sir Giles Heron, Treasurer of the Chamber, he had entered the More household in 1523, as a ward of More's on the death of his father, and had married More's daughter in 1525. He had inherited a considerable amount of property including Rycote Manor, Oxfordshire and Shakerwell Manor House in Hackney, Middlesex, where he and his family spent much of their time. It was during a visit to Shakerwell made by his father-in-law that words were said to have passed between them in the parlour, concerning the King. He was betrayed by one of his servants who had a grudge against him. In spite of a touching letter written on his behalf by his sons, to Cromwell, he was hanged, drawn and quartered at Tyburn on 4 August 1540. [176] Following hard on the tragedy came another, and one which was to come even closer to Dame Alice. It was the arrest and condemnation of her second grandson John Elrington, who had become involved in the affair known as a Plot of the Prebendaries of Canterbury against Cranmer's administration of monies due to them, and their use to spread *'new fangelled'* doctrines, and even heresies, in the county of Kent. This was of great concern to Dame Alice, as she and More had been made members of the Fraternity of Christ Church, Canterbury, in 1530, for their devotion to St Thomas à Becket and the Cathedral. As well as John Elrington, a great many of the More family and associates were involved, including John More, who was his cousin, William Dauncey, William Roper, John Heywood who had married More's niece Joan Rastell, John Larke, the Rector of Chelsea, Germain Gardiner, and John Ireland, who was the Ropers' chaplain at Well Hall, Eltham.

The King gave Cranmer a free hand to deal with the matter, and the accused were all put into custody in the Tower, and the Oath of Supremacy put before them to sign. Larke, Gardiner and Ireland all refused and probably John Elrington as well, More, Dauncey and Heywood eventually signed and were released. In the State papers of Henry VIII for 1544, the last mention of this courageous grandson of Dame Alice is made, in the pardon for John More:

> *'John More of Chelsea, Middlesex, alias of Barnborough, Yorkshire, alias of London. Pardon of all treasonable words with the detestable traitors, John Elrington, Germain Gardiner, John Bekynsale, John Heywood, William Dauncey, John Ireland, Roger Ireland and any others in wishing ill of the king, arguing against the King's Supremacy, and all concealments of treason of which he has been accused; with restoration of goods.*
> *Greenwich 24th.'*[177]

Margaret Roper, worn out with all the family troubles and sorrows died just before Christmas, in 1544, and originally her body was supposed to have been buried in the More vault at Chelsea. She left More's head to her daughter Elizabeth, who became the wife of Edward Bray, on the death of Mary Elrington, Alice's granddaughter, who was his first wife. On Elizabeth's death in 1560, More's head was buried in the Roper vault at St Dunstan's, Canterbury. Roper had always wished to be buried with his wife in Chelsea, but he was, in fact, buried in St Dunstans, and there is recent evidence to assume that he had Margaret's body removed to Canterbury as well.

In his biography of his great grandfather, Cresacre More points out that after paying off More's debts, John More had little money left of his own. Unlike his brothers-in-law, he had no profession, and was dependant on the wealth of his wife Anne. More's property of Gobions, that he should have inherited on his father's death, remained in his stepgrandmother's possession until just before her death in 1545, when it was confiscated by the Crown. On John's death, two years later, in 1547, Queen Mary restored it to his widow. It reverted to Queen Elizabeth in 1557, and was not inhabited by the family again until 1603.[178]

It is not known exactly how long Dame Alice remained in the Great House. Although, as we have seen, Sir William Paulet was granted custody of it in 1537, there is no indication that he ever lived in it, although his son, the second Marquis of Winchester, died there in 1576. What is certain is that after the death of John Larke, in 1544, Dame Alice was given the lease of a house in Chelsea, and according to Faulkner, in his *History of Chelsea,* the house was the Rectory, that had been part of More's property, and occupied by John Larke.[179] The lease was for twenty one years, which, if she had lived, would have made her nearly ninety years old when it terminated. At least she was able to stay in the house for the rest of her life if she wanted to. That she remained very much the Lady of the Manor is evident by the fact that the More Chapel in Chelsea parish church was called Lady More's Chapel in 1552, when the King's Commissioners made an inventory of all the church's possessions. Amongst other articles in the chapel was an altarcloth of Brydges (Bruges) satin, (maybe brought over by More), with a border of the same, and two curtains of silk belonging to the same, perhaps the property of her first husband, the silk mercer, or from her grandfather Sir Peter Ardern's inheritance.[180]

John More with his wife and children continued to live in Chelsea, with Dame Alice, until John's death in 1547, at the age of thirty seven.[181] Anne Cresacre finally returned to Barnborough in 1559, and married a Yorkshire neighbour of hers, George West, nephew of Sir William West. It was a long gap of widowhood for such an eligible lady, but she may have delayed her permanent return to her Yorkshire estates until after the death of her stepmother-in-law. In the following year her daughter by John More married George West's son, John, by a previous marriage. One of their descendants married a Sackville, and founded the Sackville-West family. Anne died on 2 December 1577, and is buried in St Peter's Church, Barnborough.[182]

In 1549, when the First Prayer Book of Edward VI was introduced, the Clements and Rastells fled to Louvain, followed by More's old friend Bonvisi. During all these tragic years, it must have been a great comfort to Dame Alice to think of her daughter and her husband, and the younger grandchildren, living a stable life in Horseheath Hall.

As she was eight years senior to her husband, Lady Alice must have expected him to outlive her. Neither of them would have envisaged that eleven years after his death, she would still be very much alive. The following fascinating entry, in a list of documents stamped with His Highness's secret stamp by William Clerk, in the presence of Sir Anthony Dennye, Knight, during January, 1546, reads as follows:

'Letter to Alice More, widow, in favour of Roland Hunt,
Groom of the Chamber for marriage. At the request of Mr Hare'
Letters and papers of Henry VIII, No 148/124.

As the widow of Sir Thomas More, Knight, attainted, Lady Alice was a pensioner of the King, and any possible suitor for her hand would have to obtain permission from the King to marry her. The only other Alice More known to have been in a similar position, was Alice's stepmother-in-law, Lady Alice, the widow of Sir John More. As mentioned before, she died in 1545, and was buried at Northaw, Hertfordshire. Roland Hunt's connection with the Court was probably on an honorary basis, and the title Groom of the Chamber did not imply that he was a permanent member of the Household. These honorary posts were often held by members of a livery company, and often members of the Mercer's company. Although there is no mention of a Roland Hunt as a member of the Mercer's Company, there was a Richard Hunt who was an active member in the 1520's. The Hunt family of Boreatton, Shropshire, have Roland as a family name occuring in their pedigree for four hundred years, and were also connected with the Gascoigne family who were connections of the Stockeld Middletons. The Mr Hare mentioned in the extract was Nicholas Hare, who was acting as Master of Requests at the time.

The available evidence fairly firmly established the fact that the Lady Alice was sought again in marriage at the age of 71. That she did not marry Mr Hunt is confirmed by another mention of her being involved, as Lady Alice More, in her property at Hatfield in 1548 found in the Manorial Court Roll at Hatfield. This states that *'Domina Alicia More vidua',* Sir John's widow, paid a fine regularly at the manor court from 1536 to her death in 1546, but that *'Domina le More'* paid 12d in 1548. Thus although Sir John's widow was dead, Lady Alice was still able to collect rents from their joint property, on the payment of the fine and was still known as Lady More.[183]

Lady Alice went on to outlive More by seventeen years. Her daughter Alice and her husband Sir Giles Alington continued to live at Horseheath, Sir Giles ever ready to assist her with her affairs. Of her three Elrington grandchildren, two were alive and well married into the famous Bray family, lords of the manor of Chelsea, Eaton Bray and Shere Vachery. They were Thomas Elrington, married to Beatrix Bray, daughter of Sir Edward Bray, and Mary, as previously mentioned married to her brother, also Edward, and heir to the Bray Estates.

Her nine Alington children were still alive, Richard, the second son, living as a lawyer in London, member of his stepgrandfather's Inn, Lincolns Inn. Of her stepchildren and their husbands, Margaret and John were dead, Elizabeth Dauncey was alive, and her husband William was still alive in1545 when he inherited property from his father, also Cecily Heron as far as we know.

There is of course no indication on the tomb at Chelsea as to the exact date of Lady Alice's death; the Chelsea parish registers do not commence until 1559. The apparent absence of a will would be due to the fact that on her death, her fortune from John Middleton, being in trust for her daughter Alice, would have passed straight to her and any land held as the wife of More, would, on her death, pass to the King due to his Attainder. But the year of her death has now been discovered through an entry in the Land Revenue Miscelleny, Book 216, in the Public Record Office and dated 25 April 1551:

> *'That 9s 5d of yearly rent lately paid out of one farm called Waltrottes is now*
> *withdrawn as they suppose by the same reason the same farm has now come into*
> *the King's hands by the attainder of the late Sir Thomas More,*
> *and now by the death of my Lady More his wife.*
> *That whereas 8s 2d of yearly rent was due to the Lady of his manor out of the*
> *lands and tenements lately Cranewelles and before Lavehams they*
> *say that Nicholas Lavenham held one parcel of land lying in Stokehide lately*
> *Cranewelle's sold to Sir Thomas More, now come to the King's hands*
> *by the death of the said Lady More; the rent is two shillings and tenpence.'*

The fact that the chapel in Chelsea was affectionately known around the time of her death as Lady More's Chapel, coupled with the fact that the lease of the property she lived in Chelsea had several years to run at the time of her death, leads us to assume that she died in that parish, and was buried in the vault, near the body of Jane Colt, where her husband had intended her to lie. Whether More's body was taken from its first resting place in St Peter's ad Vincula in the Tower, to Chelsea, when the fortunes of the More family were temporarily restored by the Catholic Queen Mary on coming to the throne in 1533, is still a matter of conjecture, but both Aubrey and Weever do state that More was buried in Chelsea Church, near the middle of the south wall.

But for a disturbing letter to the *Times* 11 May 1935, one would hope that at last More and his two loved wives were united, as he had hoped, in the tomb that he had made for them. But Reginald Blunt, whose father was Rector of Chelsea Old Church in 1872, relates the following strange story opposite:

*'If we are to accept Aubrey's statement
that More's body was interred in Chelsea
Church near the middle of the south wall,
this would seem to point to a western
extension of the More Chapel when the
present nave was entirely rebuilt in 1670.
Now it happens that just at the spot so
indicated a new heating chamber was
made in 1872; and in excavating for this
a vault containing several coffins was
unexpectedly broken into. The workmen
in some consternation came to my father,
who was rector at the time, to ask what
was to be done; and by his orders, the
coffins, to the number of nine, were
loaded into a van and taken to St Luke's
Church, and there bricked up in a vacant
vault, I am afraid, without any search for
name places. Rumour, I know — but
probably ex post facto rumour — had it
that one of the coffins was much shorter
than the rest'.*

If this story is true, and the coffin so much shorter than the rest contained the headless body of More, then the three of them made a last journey across the King's road, northward, and are buried somewhere in St Luke's Church, in an unmarked grave.

A Dainty Race of Children

'I never saw such a dainty race of children in all my life'
JAMES HOWELL WRITING ABOUT LADY ALICE MORE'S
GREAT-GRANDCHILDREN

O N LOOKING into the descendants of St Thomas More, we find people who have for the most part remained true to the Catholic faith, quiet landed gentry, priests and nuns, but few if any have achieved eminence in any particular field. One of the exceptions was George Eyston, racing driver, and at one time in his life *'the fastest man on earth'*. Those who had the privilege of knowing this courgeous, kindly modest man, staunch in his faith, and a great friend, can say with certainty that he had inherited many of the great qualities of his famous, saintly ancestor, a man More would have been proud to call a member of his family.

Lady Alice More's descendants all come from her daughter Alice, the only surviving child of her marriage to John Middleton. They emerge as possessing a dazzling array of talent, wealth and sometimes eccentricity, whose names have become household words. They rank amongst their number great scholars, highborn aristocrats, politicians and Queens.

Alice, first as the wife of Thomas Elrington, and then as the wife of Sir Giles Alington, gave Lady Alice More twelve grandchildren, three Elringtons and nine Alingtons. Mary Elrington was the eldest, born in 1520, four years before her grandmother and step grandfather moved out of the Old Barge at Bucklersbury to the great house at Chelsea.

The first three years of her life were divided between the family home in Willesden, and their house in Hitchin, which contained furnishings given to the young Elringtons by More.[184] Her father died when she was three in 1523, and the following year, when her mother married Sir Giles Alington, she and her

Portrait of an unknown gentlewoman, by Hans Holbein, possibly Lady Alice Alington,
daughter of Lady More / by kind permission of the British Museum.

1. Margaret = Sir RICHARD = 2. Joan Troughton
daughter of John Sandes *buried in Worcester Cathedral*

Sir JOHN

Sir REGINALD = Catherine Husse
Knight of the Garter of Eaton Bray. Lord of Manor of Chelsea. Built St. George's Chapel, Windsor, and Henry VII's Chapel, Westminster Abbey. Acquired Manor of Shere Vachery in 1497 d. 1503 (d.s.p.s.)

MARGERY = William Sandys
Baron Sandys of the Vine. Acquired Manor of Chelsea by deed of Arrangement from Edmund Bray in 1510

Lord JOHN = Anne,
d. 1557 *daughter of Francis Earl (d.s.p.s.) Buried in of Shrewsbury Chelsea Church*

REYNOLD *of Middle Temple admitted 1565, called 1574, d. 1577 d.v.p.*

two brothers Thomas and John moved to the mansion of Horseheath Hall, near Cambridge. Here Mary spent the rest of her childhood, until her marriage to Edward Bray.

The Arderns and the Harpers of Markhall and Latton had long been friends of the Bray family, and we see the hand of Dame Alice in this marriage of her eldest granddaughter, when she married Edward Bray, great nephew and heir of Sir Reginald Bray. Sir Reginald had been an associate of Sir Richard Harper, and had been named in his will as his executor, and as a beneficiary.[185] Sir Reginald Bray, Knight of the Garter, of Eton Bray, Bedfordshire, was a statesman and

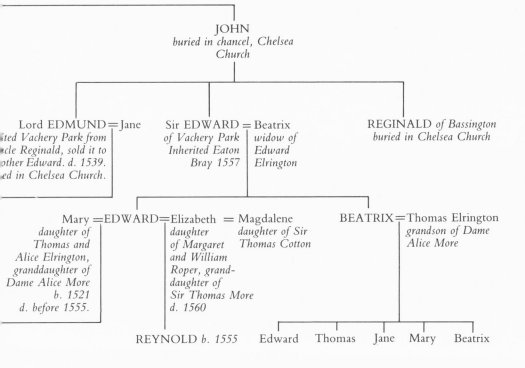

Lady Alice's descendants through the Bray & Elrington families

JOHN
buried in chancel, Chelsea Church

Lord EDMUND = Jane
...ted Vachery Park from ...cle Reginald, sold it to ...other Edward. d. 1539. ...ed in Chelsea Church.

Sir EDWARD = Beatrix
of Vachery Park | widow of Inherited Eaton | Edward Bray 1557 | Elrington

REGINALD *of Bassington buried in Chelsea Church*

Mary = EDWARD = Elizabeth = Magdalene
daughter of Thomas and Alice Elrington, granddaughter of Dame Alice More b. 1521 d. before 1555.

daughter of Margaret and William Roper, granddaughter of Sir Thomas More d. 1560

daughter of Sir Thomas Cotton

BEATRIX = Thomas Elrington
grandson of Dame Alice More

REYNOLD *b. 1555*

Edward   Thomas   Jane   Mary   Beatrix

architect. Two great monuments to his talents are St George's Chapel, Windsor, and the Henry VII Chapel in Westminster Abbey. He was also Lord of the Manor of Chelsea, and of Shere Vachery in Surrey. He died in 1503, without heirs, and his estates first went to his eldest nephew, Lord Edmund Bray. Lord Edmund sold off the Shere Vachery estates which included the house of Baynards, to his younger brother Sir Edward Bray. Edward Bray, the younger, the son of Sir Edward Bray of Vachery became Mary's husband, in 1535, the year of More's death, when she was fourteen years old.[186] The first year of her marriage must have been clouded by the tragedy of her step grandfather's tragic execution. At Baynards she gave birth to the son and heir presumptive to the Bray fortune, in 1536. He was called Reynold. He never married, and died before his father in 1577 without issue. When his cousin, Lord John Bray, son of his grandfather, Sir Edmund Bray, died without issue Sir Edward Bray senior, inherited the mansion of Eaton Bray. One of the most moving pieces of sixteenth century reporting is the account of the funeral of Lord John Bray.[187] It was the last heraldic funeral cortège to travel up the Thames on two black draped barges from the steps of Blackfriars Bridge to the landing stage at Chelsea, which More had used so often. The chief mourners included Garter and Richmond Heralds, and Mary's husband, Edward Bray.

The sombre scene in Chelsea Church, with the Chancel draped with black velvet, and the banners with the hatchments of the Bray family hanging above it, and the glittering candles, must have made a moving background to this great funeral. More's simple epitaph could be seen in the More chapel on the right of the chancel, and the open tomb of the Bray family on the left, ready for the coffin of Lord John. By the time of this funeral, Lady Alice's granddaughter Mary Bray was dead, and her husband was even more closely related to the More family through his second wife. She was Margaret and William Roper's eldest daughter, Elizabeth, More's eldest granddaughter. The Bray tomb still stands in the chancel of Chelsea Old Church today, in a very dilapidated condition, in comparison with the much restored More monument opposite it.

Elizabeth Bray also lived at Baynards. She is supposed to have kept the head of More, which had been left her by her mother, in a casket under the stairs. Her only son, also called Reynold, was born in 1555, and owing to the death of his half-brother Reynold, he ultimately inherited the Bray estates and is the ancester of the Bray's living at Shere. Edward inherited Eaton Bray in 1558, and Elizabeth died there on 21 April 1560. The record of her death is still to be seen in the parish register.[188]

The old house of Baynards was sold to Sir George More, of Loosely, a kinsman of Sir John More's third wife, in 1558. He largely rebuilt it. It was badly damaged by fire in 1979, and subsequently pulled down. But the impressive drive to the house, which was so admired by John Evelyn as *'Being one of the goodliest avenues of oaks'* that he had ever seen, is still there.

The elder of Mary's two brothers, Thomas Elrington, was born the year after her, in 1522 and at the age of two he became heir to a large part of his father's estate which included the manor of Denecourt, near Brenzett, Kent, the manor at Willesden and the manor of Fosham, Yorkshire. After a childhood spent at Horseheath Hall, he also married into the Bray family. His wife was Beatrix

Bray, the sister of Mary's husband Edward. His father Thomas Elrington senior, that young man of '*Golden character*' so admired by Erasmus and loved by More, had had a great affection for John More. Following in his father's footsteps the young Thomas Elrington kept up this affectionate relationship with John's children, and in his will of 1566 he left his manor of Willesden to Thomas More, the second, son of John and Anne Cressacre. [189]

It was the marriage of Thomas Elrington's son Edward into the Spencer family of Althorpe that brings Lady Alice's descendants into near connection with the Princess of Wales. Edward married Margaret, daughter of Sir John Spencer, direct ancestor of the Lady Diana Spencer, Princess of Wales. Margaret had been married before, to Sir Giles Alington, old Sir Giles Alington's great grandson and heir. There is some hard feeling towards this lady in the Alington family as apart from a grey horse that she left to her son Giles Alington, all her property was left to the Elrington family.

Another of Thomas Elrington's children, Mary, married into the family of Lord Morley, who bought the old Markhall estate in Essex, home of the Arderns, from Thomas Shaa.

John, the youngest of the Elrington grandchildren must have caused Lady Alice great sorrow. He was born in 1523, just before his father's death. Deeply involved with other members of the More family and their chaplains in the Plot of the Prebendaries of Canterbury, there is no trace of him recanting, or like John More and William Dauncey, being pardoned and released after their captivity in the Tower in 1544. With John Larke, and Germain Gardiner, and John Ireland, he probably suffered at Tyburn for his faith. He would have been twenty-one. [190]

Horseheath Hall, where all the grandchildren were brought up, for all its splendour, must have been bitterly cold in winter. They say that when the wind is in the east, its biting thrust drives straight across the land between the Ural Mountains and the hill to the east of Horseheath village, which is now called Hall meadow, where the stately and beautiful home of the Alingtons stood. Until 1758, the great house only had seven fireplaces, [191] and so in the time when Lady Alice's grandchildren lived there, they must have dreaded the long dark days. In spite of this the spirit of the house was warm and hospitable, and the management of the household and children was much admired by More, and was a great tribute to More's education of his stepdaughter, and Lady Alice's good example. Austin Harvey describes the place in glowing terms:

'They beautifed the place with their stately mansion, and well timbered park.
They filled the parish church with the monuments of their dead, and made its

pavements and its windows rich with memorials in brass and glass, of the
virtues and heraldic glories of their House. [192]

The beauty of the grounds, the splendour of the apartments and the careful education of the children in their religious and academic studies, on the lines More had laid down for his own school in Bucklersbury and Chelsea, made it a fitting place to carry on the traditions of those remarkable households. Margaret Roper, always a close friend of Alice Alington, brought her family there to stay for long periods, and at one time suggested to Roger Ascham, who later became tutor to Princess Elizabeth, that he should become tutor to the Horseheath children. [193] In view of his strong protestant leanings this was an odd request, and he turned the offer down, perhaps because he did not wish to be involved with More's family so soon after his death.

We can catch a glimpse of the wealth of the Horseheath household by reading Sir Giles Alington's will. [194] As official cupbearer to the King, he had inherited from his forebears a wonderful collection of silver, and had added to it during his own tenure of office, by his services at Henry VIII's wedding to Anne Boleyn, and various other Royal occasions. One of his more amusing acquisitions was an enormous copper gilt ball which he brought back with him from the Siege of Boulogne, in 1544, as a memento of the battle. The top was sawn off, turning the bell into a giant goblet, which held sixty gallons of wine, and must have caused much merriment amongst the family. When Horseheath Hall was rebuilt, it was placed on top of the cupola of the house where it remained until the house was demolished in 1777. It was purchased by Mr George Ashby, of Naseby, and placed on the spire of the parish church, and was known for many years as the *'old man of Naseby'*. It can still be seen lying inside the church. There is nothing to identify it to the passing visitors, who think it is a relic of the last great battle of the Civil War. Lady Alice, on her visits to Horseheath must have seen it and probably had a drink out of it.

Amongst the splendid family jewels that were worn by Alice Alington were such pieces as a gold pomadore, a gold tablet enamelled with pearls, a jewel with a unicorn, a great chain with pearls, a hoop of gold, a sapphire ring, a turquoise ring, a jewel with an agate garnished with four diamonds, and a flower of diamonds. Such finery, worn by her daughter, must have gladdened the heart of the dress-conscious mother.

Of all the grandchildren at Horseheath, perhaps it was Richard Alington, the second son of Sir Giles and Alice, who seems to have suffered the greatest shock at the death of More, which was to affect him profoundly for the rest of his life. He had been very aware of his mother's efforts to save More's life, and he would have read the letter from the Tower written by More and Margaret Roper to her. Even at the age of ten he would have understood what courage was sometimes needed to remain *the King's good servant, but God's first',* just as his stepgrandfather was doing. He writes of his childhood at Horseheath, and of the strange visions he had as a child, from the time of More's death, when he was ten, until the age of thirteen:

> *When I was a child I was brought up with a good father and mother, who duly used us children virtuislie, and kept us for one hour or two every day and morning to prayers; and then when prayers was done to our books. And afterwards we were wont to go to play into an orchard near by adjoining unto my father's house, where as often times for the space of three years there appeared unto me, in a thick hedge, a goodlie and comfortable vision. I well remember from ten years old unto thirteen, there appeared to me the very image of Our Saviour, Jesus Christ, as he suffered his blessed passion upon the Cross, which image appeared unto me very lively, and that very often, so loving and tender as ever any earthly man would desire or wish, which I did ever more keep very secret unto myself, for my great comfort and consolation.* [195]

Richard would have been about seventeen when his half-brother, John Elrington, and other members of the family became involved in the Plot of the Prebendaries of Canterbury, and John's conviction and death must have been the cause of great sorrow to the Horseheath household, and particularly to this sensitive, imaginative boy. He went to London to study law at Lincoln's Inn, and became a lawyer and, by his own account, a shrewd and not too scrupulus money-lender. He married Jane, the sister of Sir William Cordell, Master of the Rolls. He had three daughters by her. The preponderance of women in the family of Lady Alice is remarkable, even for a time when mortality of male children was so much higher than of female. Sir Peter Ardern only had daughters, Alice and John Middleton likewise, and this remarkable grandson of Lady Alice again had no male heir. Of his three daughters, two survived, Cordell and Mary.

By his late thirties he became, after a lapse of some years, a deeply religious man, counting amongst his friends such staunch Catholics as Abbot Feckenham, the last Catholic Abbot of Westminster Abbey, Doctor Scott, the Bishop of Chester, Dr Cole, the Dean of St Pauls, and Mr Boxhall of New College, and Warden of Winchester. Richard suffered from the age in which he lived, when allegiance to the Crown brought conflict with faith: During the reign of Queen Mary he would have had a respite from this dilemma, and it is apparent that on the accession of Elizabeth he once again found the conflict undermining his health and even his sanity. By June 1561 he was gravely ill and drew up his will in his own hand, which has a beautiful little drawing by him of a crucifix in the margin.[196] By this time his great friends, Feckenham among them, had been imprisoned in the Tower or the Fleet for their refusal to comply with the laws of the Church of England. William Roper was a staunch friend of Feckenham, as was Thomas Pope, More's *'singular friend'*. In his will Richard left a large sum of money to Cordell, Roper, Feckenham, Boxhall, Cole and Scott *'to be devoted to a lively remembrance of the Passion and death of Christ'*, to be provided either daily or weekly.

Was this Richard's way of asking his friends to say Masses for the repose of his soul, without incriminating them in any way, or had he some permanent building of a large crucifix in mind? I think the first answer is the more likely although there is one strange entry in the biography of Abbot Feckenham in the *D.N.B.* It states that, while a prisoner in Wisbech Castle during the last years of his life, he devoted his time to building a cross.

Richard Alington's tomb can still be seen by paying a visit to one of the smallest, least known, but most fascinating museums in London. It lies in Chancery Lane, behind the pinnacled Victorian facade of the Public Record Office, and stands on the site of the Chapel of the Rolls. In the sixteenth century the Chapel was not only part of the house of the Master of the Rolls, and used for worship by him and members of his family, but it was used as a supplmentary repository for the rolls and records of Chancery. In 1895, as part of a scheme to extend the Record Office, the chapel was pulled down, but some of its finest monuments and glass were incorporated in the new building. Amongst these Richard Alington's monument and the vault beneath were given pride of place in the museum, and there is a photo of it on the front cover of their excellent catalogue.

The tomb is made of alabaster, and he is seen kneeling opposite Jane, his wife, with his three small daughters kneeling beneath them. The arms of the Stockeld Middletons are clearly seen on the large coat of arms at the base, a reminder of his grandfather, Lady Alice's first husband, John Middleton. She did not live long enough to see the last tragic illness of her grandson, and if she had known about his visions, her sound, down to earth commonsense would have strongly advised him not to give way to such religious fantasies. Alice, his mother, was a deeply pious woman, and lived to see this son of hers suffer so much from his tortured conscience. She died two years after him in 1563.

She was buried in Horseheath Church, in an elaborate tomb which was made for her and Sir Giles, who was buried there twenty-one years after her. It stands in the south part of the chancel, and used to have an elaborate canopy over it with a great blazoning of arms, including those of her father, John Middleton. This superstructure was removed in 1883, to allow more light to enter the church from the window behind it. The effigies of her and her children have also gone, leaving her husband Sir Giles only, lying on the tomb, with his father beneath him. The Middleton arms can be seen on the tomb of Sir Giles' great grandson, another Giles Alington, wrongly, in fact, as he was only Alice's step-great-grandson.

Richard was obviously very highly thought of, not only by his family and legal associates, but by the Catholic clerical fraternity. Even thirteen years after his death his remarkable visions were still talked of in London and Douay by such distinguished priests as Bishop Allen, whose college in London stands today on the sight of the More House in Chelsea, in the middle of Beaufort Street. Father Richard Bristow was one of the most renowned Catholics of his day, and was appointed by Doctor Allen to be prefect of studies in his new college at Douay. He writes of Richard in his book *A Brief Treatise of divers plain and sure ways to find out the truth in this doubtful and dangerous time of Heresy*, written in 1574:

> *'As for the strange and miraculous vision of Mr Alington, I say nothing of it, as it is a thing famously known, the witnesses also well known men of great worship and as yet living. If any man that hath not heard it be desirous to know how, and what it was, he may by a little enquiry in London come to the knowledge of it'.*

Sir William Cordell survived his brother-in-law by nineteen years. He had accumulated a large fortune, and acquired the beautiful property of Long Melford Hall in Suffolk in 1547. He had been intimate with the Alington family for many years, and was made executor of Sir Giles Alington's will in 1569. Old Sir Giles, in fact, outlived him, dying at the remarkable age of eighty six, in 1586. Sir William died without children, and Richard's widow inherited Long Melford. Two of Richard and Jane's three daughters survived childhood, and it was Lady Alice's great granddaughter Mary who inherited Long Melford from her mother.[197] The house which stands today much as it did in the late sixteenth and early seventeenth century, was to be the home of two of Lady Alice's great grandchildren, Richard's daughter Mary, and her husband Sir John Savage. John was the son of the marriage between Margaret, Lady Alice's youngest

Alington granddaughter, and Sir John Savage of Rock Savage, Clifton. Young John was one of Sir Giles Alington's favourite grandsons, and in his will he left him a gilt standing cup used when drinking sack, to show his natural affection for him.

Their son Thomas, Alice's great great grandson, also inherited Melford and became the first Viscount Savage of Rock Savage, in 1626. He married Elizabeth daughter of Viscount Rivers. On her father's death she became Countess Rivers in her own right, and added Hengrave Hall to the families' great territorial possessions. The household of children at Long Melford was greatly admired by James Howell, who tutored them in Spanish for a short time, and maintained a correspondence with them all for many years:

'I live in so civil and noble a family, as virtuous and regular a house as any, I believe in the land, both for economical government and for choice of company — for I never saw yet such a dainty race of children in all my life'. [198] The family had Alice's blood on both sides and had inherited many of her excellent qualities.

He particularly admired Jane Savage, who like her great great grandmother Alice Alington, was a girl of *'dazzling beauty'!* As Erasmus had sung the praises of Alice, so, a hundred years later, both Milton and Ben Johnson were to immortalize this great great granddaughter, who became the wife of the fifth Marquis of Winchester, in deeply moving poems they wrote, on hearing of her death in childbirth at the age of twenty-three. She had already given birth to a son and heir, Charles, but never lived to see the outstanding courage that her husband showed when his house at Basing was to withstand one of the greatest sieges of the Civil War. Like so many of Lady Alice's descendants, they were staunch Catholics and devoted to the Royalist cause. Milton's epitaph on Jane begins thus:

'This rich marble doth inter
The honour'd wife of Winchester,
A Viscounts daughter, an Earls heir,
Besides what her virtues fair
Added to her noble birth,
More than she could own from Earth,
Summers three times eight says one
She had told, alas, too soon,
After so short time of breath,
To house with darkness and with death.
Yet had the number of her days

Rock Savage / reproduced by kind permission of Lord Cholmondeley.

Bin as complete as was her praise,
Nature and fate had had no strife
In giving limit to her life.
Her high birth, and her graces sweet,
Quickly found a lover meet;
The virgin quire for her request
The God that Sits at marriage feast;
He at their invoking came
But with a scarce-well-lighted flame;'

Ben Johnson's Elergie on her is equally beautiful:

'What gentle Ghost, besprent with April dew
Hayles me so solomely to yonder yewgh,
And beckoning wooes me from the fatal tree
To pluck a garland for herself or me?
I doe obey you, Beauty, for in death
You seem a faire one, O that you had breath
To give your shade a name, Stay, stay, I feel
A horror in me, all my blood is steele,
Stiff, starke! my joints 'gainst one another knock,
Whose daughter?, ha!, great Savage of the Rock?
He's good, as great. I am almost a stone,
Ane ere I can ask more of her she's gone!

Her sweetness, softness, her faire courtesie,
Her wary guards, her wise simplicity,
Were like a ring of virtues bout her set
And pretty the centre where all met.

She comforted her Lord, and blest her son,
Cheered her faire sisters in her race to run
With gladness tempered her sad parents tears,
Made her friends joys to get above their fears.
And in her last act, taught the Standers by,
With admiration and applause to die!'

It was the first Marquis of Winchester who took over the Mores' Great House at Chelsea. By the time Lady Alice's great great granddaughter married into the Paulet family the property, had, sadly, passed out of their hands.

Sir Richard Alington's other surviving daughter, Cordell, made an equally good marriage to Sir John Stanhope, of Shelford, Nottingham. Their son, Philip, who was Lady Alice's great great grandson, was born in 1584, and became the first Earl Chesterfield. He had eleven sons by his first wife, Catherine, daughter of Francis, Lord Hastings. He was a staunch Royalist, and suffered great personal losses for the King's cause. His house of Bretby was sacked, and his son Philip was killed at the storming of his other property, Shelford House, in 1645. He had already lost his eldest son, John, in 1625, and his second son, Henry, in 1634. His fourth son, Ferdinand, who was a Colonel in the King's horse, was killed at Bridgeford in 1644. On hearing of his death, his first cousin, Sir Aston Cokayne wrote the following epitaph for him:

'Here underneath this monumental stone,
Lie Honour, Youth and Beauty all in one;
For Ferdinando Stanhope here doth rest
Of all those three the most unequalled test.
He was too handsome, and too stout to be
Met face to face by any enemy;
Therefore his foe, full for his death inclined,
Stole basely near, and shot him through, behind.'

The first Earl married for the second time to Anne, daughter of Sir John Pakington, and widow of Sir Humphrey Ferras of Tamworth Castle. He had one son, Alexander, by this marriage. Before we go on to study more closely Lady Alice's descendants from his first marriage, it is well worth meeting one of her fascinating descendants from the second, the Lady Hester Stanhope. We have already been introduced to her nose, from Lytton Strachey's description at the beginning of this book![199]

Hester was born in 1776, and was the eldest daughter of the third Earl Stanhope. She was considered brilliant rather than handsome, a woman of extremely forceful character and cheerfulness. Unhappy at home with her eccentric father, she became a great favourite of her uncle, William Pitt, and went to run his house for him until his death in 1806. In 1810 she left England for the Lebanon, and never returned. This woman had many characteristics in common with Lady Alice, apart from her nose! She was a forceful talker, great lover of animals and showed remarkable ability in running a Prime Minister's household, as well as her own extraordinary ménage in the Lebanon. There is one story of her haranguing one unfortunate man for so many hours, when he came to visit her, that he fainted away with fatigue. As was said of her ancestress,

Lady Alice and her mother, *'It is of their nature to be a little talkative!'*

Her nephew, the fifth Earl Stanhope, is remembered by all lovers of portraiture, as being the founder of the National Portrait Gallery. It was a happy co-incidence that this descendant of Lady Alice started the Gallery, where, in 1978, the exhibition to commemorate the four hundredth anniversary of her husband's death, *'The King's Good Servant'*, was presented.

To return to the first Earl Chesterfield, due to the tragedy of all his sons dying before him, his heir was his grandson, Philip, who became the second Earl in 1656. He married three times, his first wife being Anne Percy, daughter of the Earl of Northumberland. They had no children. By his second wife, Lady Elizabeth Butler, he had a daughter Elizabeth, who married John Lyon, the Fourth Earl of Strathmore. Thus the first of Lady Alice's descendants to bear this title was their son, the fifth Earl, who was killed in the Rebellion at the Battle of Sheriffmuir, in 1715.

Another of Lady Alice's direct descendants was the Fourth Earl of Chesterfield, *'The Little Earl'* as he was known by his friends, because of his height. Born in 1694, this outstanding man was a politician, wit, and letter writer. It is this last quality which is his chief claim to fame. He had no legitimate children, and overwhelmed his one illigitimate son with a series of almost daily letters in French and English, which the poor child was expected to answer to perfection, from the age of five. Chesterfield wrote to his son — *'Never were so much pains taken for anyone's education, and never had anyone so many opportunities for knowledge and improvement'*. If Lord Chesterfield had looked back at his ancestress, Lady Alice, he would have seen her presiding in a similar fashion over the daily, arduous correspondence that the children of the More household were forced to send to their father every day that he was away from them, which was sometimes not weeks, but months at a time. Lady Alice, on More's behalf, was as relentless in her direction of her stepchildren's education, and letter writing, as Lord Chesterfield was with his son, and perhaps with more success. Poor Philip Stanhope never attained the heights of perfection that his father had hoped for him.

Although the family home of the Strathmores is Glamis Castle, Angus, Scotland, one of Lady Alice's most distinguished descendants from them was born in Hertfordshire, only a mile or so from the land that she inherited from her first husband, John Middleton, at Ippolletts, outside Hitchin. On 4 August, four hundred and fifty years after her death, the youngest daughter of the fourteenth Earl was born at St Pauls Walden. She was known as Elizabeth of Glamis. She

H M Queen Elizabeth, the Queen Mother aged four, with her brother, the Hon. David Bowes-Lyon — youngest children of the Earl of Strathmore — direct descendents of Lady Alice / by kind permission of Countryside Books.

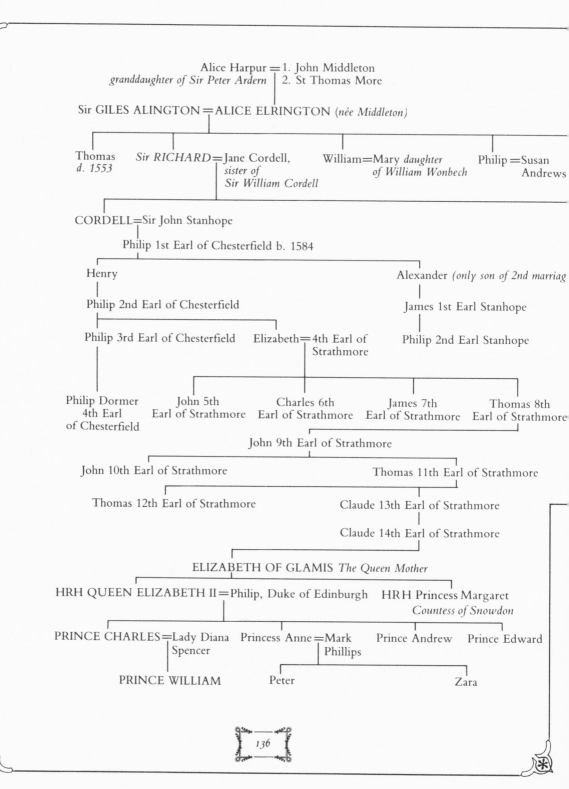

Alice Harpur = 1. John Middleton
granddaughter of Sir Peter Ardern   2. St Thomas More

Sir GILES ALINGTON = ALICE ELRINGTON (*née Middleton*)

Thomas
d. 1553

Sir RICHARD = Jane Cordell,
*sister of
Sir William Cordell*

William = Mary *daughter
of William Wonbech*

Philip = Susan
Andrews

CORDELL = Sir John Stanhope

Philip 1st Earl of Chesterfield b. 1584

Henry

Alexander *(only son of 2nd marriag*

Philip 2nd Earl of Chesterfield

James 1st Earl Stanhope

Philip 3rd Earl of Chesterfield

Elizabeth = 4th Earl of
Strathmore

Philip 2nd Earl Stanhope

Philip Dormer
4th Earl
of Chesterfield

John 5th
Earl of Strathmore

Charles 6th
Earl of Strathmore

James 7th
Earl of Strathmore

Thomas 8th
Earl of Strathmore

John 9th Earl of Strathmore

John 10th Earl of Strathmore

Thomas 11th Earl of Strathmore

Thomas 12th Earl of Strathmore

Claude 13th Earl of Strathmore

Claude 14th Earl of Strathmore

ELIZABETH OF GLAMIS *The Queen Mother*

HRH QUEEN ELIZABETH II = Philip, Duke of Edinburgh

HRH Princess Margaret
Countess of Snowdon

PRINCE CHARLES = Lady Diana
Spencer

Princess Anne = Mark
Phillips

Prince Andrew

Prince Edward

PRINCE WILLIAM

Peter

Zara

```
┌──────────┬──────────────┬───────────────┬──────────────────────────┐
Frances   Elizabeth=Robert    Jane =1. Thomas Browne of      Margaret=Sir John Savage
                  Chapman              Flambois                        of Clifton
                  of Abbington      2. John Mildmay, brother of Walter,
                  Cambs.               Founder of Emanuel Coll. Cambs.
```

Y=Sir John Savage *Inherited Long Melford Hall*

Thomas 1st Viscount Savage *of Rock Savage* =Elizabeth
    | *daughter of*

Jane = John, 5th Marquis of Winchester   *Viscount Rivers*

ALINGTON
Sable & bend
engrailed between
six billets agent

MIDDLETON
Argent fretty sable
a Canton of the
last

Lady Alice's descendants through the Alington family

married the Duke of York, second son of King George V, in 1923. On the abdication of her brother-in-law, Edward VIII, in 1936 her husband became George VI, and she Queen Consort. She was crowned in Westminster Abbey on 12 May 1937. Queen Elizabeth II, her daughter, can therefore trace her ancestry directly back to John Middleton, Merchant of the Staple of Calais, and Mercer of London, and his wife Alice. The Queen Mother has much in common with her ancestress, love of children, love of animals, a great interest in young people, a strong religious faith, a woman of great courage and tenacity in the face of much sorrow and adversity, short of stature, and a fluent and extremely amusing conversationalist.

Epilogue

'a Jollie Maister Woman'

St Thomas More. DIALOGUE OF COMFORT

THIS STUDY of Lady Alice More, who has stood beside her husband, in his shadow, for so long, not only throws a light on her, but seems to put him in a new light as well. Seen through her eyes, he comes down a little from the pedestal where he has been placed by his admirers, and is cut down to the size of a man; a man with many faults, seen by none more clearly than his wife, who had lived with him for twenty-four years. In More's tendency to religious fanaticism, of which Dame Alice so strongly disapproved, lay the root of his ultimate sanctity. The fact that sanctity was ultimately achieved, and that he remained, until the end of his life, a *'Man for all Seasons'*, is never doubted. Lady Alice, by her constant watch and care of him, by her pruning of his more excessive spiritual tendencies, by her balanced outlook on life, played a great part in the final flowering of his remarkable character.

More's first young wife was formed and moulded to his idea of what he thought his wife should be. His second was a sparring partner for him to sharpen his wits on, and she made her own powerful contribution to the style of his household in her own right. It was her dislike of what, for want of a better word, might be called More's puritanical streak, that enabled the household to be a comfortable, pleasant place to be in, not a monastic cell. Excellent housekeeper that Lady Alice was, she had her extravagances. As More pointed out in his *Dialogue of Comfort, 'she could be a penny wise, pound foolish, saving a candle end, and spoiling a velvet gown'*. It is good to hear that she had and wore her velvet gowns, and encouraged his children to wear theirs.

We also hear from her husband that she enjoyed discussions on the Church, and unlike him, who never liked to be late for a meal, she would choose to hear the arguments carried out to the end, and let the meal wait. The gulf that might have kept More apart from his wordly, practical wife was not lack of piety on her part, but dislike of it in excess, and it was bridged by their common sense of humour. Married to a great wit, Alice was no mean humorist herself, and like all good wits, she possessed a delightful capacity for turning the trials and tribulations of life into a joke. Even from the distance of over four hundred years their arguments ring with good humour, the good humour that can only exist between a husband and wife who have a deep and abiding love for each other. This dialogue of humour lasted from the happy days in the parlour at Bucklersbury, to the tragic ones in the cell in the Tower of London, where the small figure of Dame Alice, bustling in, with her taunts and jokes, must have so gladdened his heart, and raised his spirits. He may have longed for Margaret Roper's company for the intellectual conversations, but he longed for Alice's for the laughs, and no man needs to laugh more than one facing such a death.

Professor Chambers laments that Benvenuto, that master of gossips, never came to England, when he would, no doubt, have visited the Chelsea household, and given us some good chat about it, which might have dissipated that atmosphere of blamelessness which is the great difficulty with which More's biographers have to cope. I hope that this attempt to see him through the eyes of his wife may help.

Ro. Ba. refers to the ultimate destination of Dame Alice's soul in such a way, that it would have made husband and wife laugh a lot:

> *'Sir Thomas so much bettered the state of her mind, that I doubt not that she is a saved soul, and they now enjoy each others company in bliss'.*

Now knowing Dame Alice a little better, we may assume that they both assisted each other on their way to Heaven, where they are now *'right merry together'*.

ET LUX PERPETUA LUCEAT EIS.

Chapter Notes

Prologue

1 *Letters and Papers, Henry VIII*, Addenda I, i, No. 1024
2 The Life of the Blessed Thomas More, T.E. Bridgett
3 Born for Friendship, Bernard Basset

An Ardern Mystery

4 *Arderns of Warwickshire*, Burke's Landed Gentry, 1939
5 Will of John Ardern, P.C.C. Porch, 1526
   Shakespeareana Genealogica, p489
6 *Thomas More* R.W. Chambers, p339
7 *History of Cottisford* J.C. Blomfield, 1887
8 *Essex Recusant* D. Shanahan. Vol 19, p110
9 Will of John Middleton P.C.C. 22 Bennett. Oct 4. 1509
10 *History of Colt Family* by G.F.R. Colt. 1887. p232
11 Will of John Colt P.C.C. 1522. 18 Maynwaryng
12 *Letters and Papers Henry VIII*. Vol XVI. No 744
13 Elrington Pedigree Excerpta Cantiana. Thomas Streatfield
14 *Home and Counties Magazine* IV. 1902.
15 Will of Sir Peter Ardern P.C.C. 19 Godyn
16 *Morant's Essex II*. p21
17 D.N.B. Owen Tudor. Morant's Essex II. p21.
18 *Letters and Papers. Henry VIII*. ii. 29 ef p96.
19 Will of John Skreene. P.C.C. Wattys. Fol 138. 1474. Morant's Essex I. p50
20 Close Rolls. 1485. 333
21 *Transactions of Essex Archaeological Society*. New Series. Vol 7. 1898. *Gough's Maps*. 223. Plt LXXXV
22 O. Pacht. *Burlington Magazine*. LXXXIV. 1944. pp138ff
23 *John Weever's Funeral Monuments*. Vet A5 d 387
24 Richard Newcourt, *Repertorium* Vol I. p584
25 *Stowe's Survey of London*. Chelsea. III. 1921. p24–25
26 *Brief Lifes* John Aubrey. Cressent Press. MCMXLIX. p316–317
27 *Gentleman's Magazine*. 1833. Dec. p481
28 *Memorials of Old Chelsea* A. Beaver. 1982. p74
29 *Chelsea Old Church* Randall Davies. p100
30 Notes and Queries. 9th Series. IV. July 1899
31 Letter to Mrs Carwardine Probert from *East Herts Archaeological Society*. May, 1935

Mistress Alice Middleton

32 Will of Sir Richard Harpur, P.C.C. 15 Doggett. 1492
33 *Feet of Fines*. London and Middlesex. 14 Henry VII
34 Close Rolls. 1501. 62
35 *History of Latton*. Jonathan Edwards. p19
36 Will of Sir John Shaa. P.C.C. Holgrove. 1504
37 Close Rolls. 1508, 925
38 *Letters and Papers Henry VIII*. Vol 1, part I. Oct 12 1510
39 *Victoria County History*. *Middlesex*. Vol II. p225.

40   *Feet of Fines. Essex. 1527. No 366*

41   *Guide to Church of St Olav*, Hart Street.
      A. Powell-Miller

42   Will of Alice Middleton. York. Vol 4,
      fol 121v. 1474

43   *Formation and Development of a Yorkshire
      Estate, Stockeld.* A. Garnon Williams,
      University of Leeds, 1978

44   Will of Sir Peter Ardern. Ibid, Chap. 1
      note 12

45   *Genealogist* Vol 23. p38–39

46   *Hertfordshire County Records* 1 March,
      1536/7. No 87615

47   *History of Hitchin.* Reginal Hine. Vol 4.
      p358. Lay Subsidy Rolls 1504

48   *Life of Sir Thomas More.* Cresacre More.
      E.E.T.S.

Mistress Alice More

49   Harpsfield. E.E.T.S. p95

50   Ro.Ba. E.E.T.S. p113

51   Roper. E.E.T.S. p124, note 82 (8–9)

52   *Letters and Papers. Henry VIII.* 2. Part I.
      No 2726

53   Allen IV. No 999. p19

54   *Roper's Life of More.* Gollanz. p184

55   *John Clement and his Books* by A.W.
      Reed. The Library. Vol VI. No 4

56   Allen II. No 451

57   *St Thomas More and his Friends* E.M.
      Routh. p52

58   Allen I. No 451

59   P.R.O. Wolsey 546/52

60   Sir Thomas Lovell's Will. *Letters and
      Papers. Henry VIII.* vol IV. p155. 1524

61   Allen IV. 999

62   Allen IV. No 1233

The School

63   Allen IV. No 1233. Translation by Sir
      Roger Mynors for the Toronto Uni-
      versity Press edition of *Erasmus' Letters*

64   Elrington Pedigree. *Excerpta Cantiana.*
      Thomas Streatfield

65   *History of Hertfordshire.* J.E. Cussons.
      1874. p43

66   Ibid. note 1

67   Rogers 63. (ed 1947)

68   Rogers 57. (ed 1947)

69   *Pevsner's Hertfordshire.* p96

70   Rogers 69. (ed 1947)

71   Rogers 106–8. (ed 1947)

72   Harpsfield. pp93–4

73   Ro.Ba. 113

74   Harpsfield. p84

75   Ibid. note 1

Lady Alice More

76   Sir Thomas Lovell. D.N.B.

77   Will of Thomas Elrington. P.C.C. 16
      Bodfelde
      P.R.O. Chancery Innings. p.m. II Vol
      40. No 29 Kent. Thomas Elrington.
      Sir John More, Kt, one of his feoffees,
      Sir Thomas More another, 20 Sept, 8
      Henry VIII, on his wife Alice Middle-
      ton, dau. of Alice More, wife of Sir
      Thomas More. Elrington's will made
      at Chelsey, 22 Sept, 1523 (recited), on
      which day he died there. Thomas, his
      son and heir by said Alice, then aet 3.
      This entry raises the point that the
      Mores might already have moved to
      Chelsea by 1523, as Thomas Elrington
      died there. He does not appear to have
      owned any property there himself.
      There is a note in the late Mrs Carwar-
      dine Probert's papes which states that
      'Lady More had lands of her own in
      London in 1522, valued at 100 marks'.
      It was taken down in the British
      Museum, but, alas, no reference
      given, and so far I have been unable to
      trace it.

78   Works. 1557. p1434–43

79   *Records of Treasury Receipts.* P.R.O.E.
      405, No 480

80   Will of 1st Sir Giles Alington. P.C.C.
      Porch f 14

81   *Cambridge Antiquarian Society.* Vol XLI.
      1943–1947, Horseheath Hall and its
      Owners by Catherine Parsons

82   *Dialogue of Comfort.* Works, 1557, p1170

83   *Feet of Fines Essex.* 1514. No 38

84   Richard Fermor. D.N.B.

85   *Richard Grafton* by J. Kingdom. 1908.
        Add pXXI
86   *Harleian Society* Pub. Vol XXV, p4, 161.
        1520
87   Ibid. Chap. IV. note 1

The Great House at Chelsea

88   *The Field is Won.* E.M. Reynolds. p181.
        Note 5
89   Will of John Colt. P.C.C. 18 Mayn-
        waryng. 1522
90   *The Likeness of Thomas More.* Stanley
        Morison. p20
91   Allen VII. Nos 2211, 2212
92   Roper. p82
93   *Some Famous Buildings and their Story*
        A.W. Chapman. Chap 6
94   *Moreana.* Vol XII. 47–48
95   Hatfield House Archives. (C.P.M.II/9,
        10)
96   *Memorials of Old Chelsea.* A. Beaver.
        p120. 'Il Moro'. Ellis Heywood. 1556
97   Ro.Ba. p113
98   Works. Sept 3rd, 1529. (1557). p1419
99   Allen. Dec 15th. 1516. No 502
100 *Confutation of Tyndale's Answer.* Works,
        1557. p193

The Calm

101 Bodleian. ms. Land 597, fol 31b
102 Roper. pp32–33
103 *Hall's Chronicle.* ed Whibley. II. pp164–5
104 D.N.B. George Cavendish. *Life and
        Death of Cardinal Wolsey.* E.E.T.S.
        pxviii notes
105 *The King's Good Servant.* Catalogue.
        National Portrait Gallery. No 281
106 P.R.O. *Land Revenue Misc.* Book 216.
        April 25, 1551
107 Roper. p55
108 Roper. pp55–6

The Storm

109 *The Field is Won.* E.E. Reynolds. p255
110 *Hatfield and its People.* W.E.A. Book 2.
        1960. pp10, 11
111 Roper. pp52–55

112 Ibid
113 *Cresacre More.* p205
114 *John More's Book of Hours.* Notes and
        Queries. 8th Series. (121–2)
115 Roper. p48
116 Ibid. note 110
117 Apologye. p51
118 D.N.B. Hans Holbein
119 Roper. pp71–72
120 Bridgett. p121
121 Original Indenture, March 25, 1534.
        Charters Mdx. 90/ London. Ch. Musc
        a. 2 Moreana. Vol XVI. Tome 2. 1979
122 Roper. p73
123 Roper. p74–5

The Prisoner's Wife

124 Works. 1557. p1430
125 Tower charges for prisoners, compiled
        1539. British Museum
126 *Dialogue of Comfort.* p385
127 Ibid
128 *Guide to the Tower of London.* Olwen
        Hedley. Pitkin
129 Roper. p84
130 Works. 1557. p1431
131 Ibid
132 D.N.B. Thomas Audley. 1448–1544
133 Works. 1557. p1434 *Letters and Papers.
        Henry VIII.* 1113. (1534)
134 Ibid
135 Works. 1557. 1434–43
136 Ibid

A Deep Rooted Scruple

137 *Letters and Papers. Henry VIII.* Vol VII.
        1591
138 Charges for Prisoners in Tower, com-
        piled in 1537. British Museum
139 *Letters and Papers. Henry VIII.* Vol VII.
        1591
140 The manor of South was a reward to
        More from the King in 1522, after the
        execution of the Duke of Buckingham
        Letters and Papers Henry VIII. Vol
        III. No 2239

141 *Letters and Papers. Henry VIII.* Vol III 800 Howard's Letts. p271

142 Rogers 215 *Letters and Papers. Henry VIII.* Vol III 800

143 *Conscience Decides.* Letter IV. p70

144 Ibid

145 Ibid. p63

146 Ibid. p67–8

147 Works. 1557. p1432

A Matter of Conscience

148 *History of St Thomas of Acon.* J. Watney. 1892

149 Will of Sir John Shaa. P.C.C. 13 Holgrove. Fol 98–100. 1504

150 *History of Latton.* Jonathan Edwards. p19

151 *Letters and Papers. Henry VIII.* ii 29. p96

152 Will of Sir Peter Ardern. P.C.C. 19 Godyn

153 P.R.O. SP/2/R. Folio 24 & 25 *Letters and Papers. Henry VIII.* Vol VII. No 814, 2, ii

154 Roper. E.E.T.S. p87–8

155 a. D.N.B. Richard Rich
b. George Harpur, grand-son of Sir Richard Harpur, nephew of Lady Alice had his manor of Passelow alienated to Richard Rich in 1541. Morant Vol I. p50
c. The Southwell properties of Badow Hall, and Filiols (Felix Hall), Essex, were also alienated to Richard Rich in 36 *Henry VIII. Letters and Papers,* 36. p41. They had come to Southwell through Anne Bohun, eldest daughter of Sir Peter Ardern.

156 Harpsfield. p193

157 Roper. p97

158 Works. 1557. p1437
'*Lady Conyers*', Conyers was the name of Bishop Tunstall's mother. He was the illegitimate son of Thomas Tunstall, of Thurland Castle, Lancs. He was not able to visit More in the Tower, and may have sent this relative instead.
'*She sued hither this day*', Probably through Dame Alice, who would have mentioned the trouble to him on her last visit.
'*Algorism stone*', Counters for working out arabic numerals.

Comforter of all Sorrows

159 *Trinity College, Oxford.* H.E. Blakiston. p50

160 Roper. 100–2

161 Ibid

162 *Paris News Letter,* 1535
Harpsfield p253–266
Bibliotheque Nationale, Paris. Cabinet des Manuscrits (Mss franç 2981 f1 44–45)

163 Chambers p350

164 Harpsfield. p209

165 Stapleton. p192

166 *History of England.* Macaulay Vol I. Chap V 306. (Longman & Green)

Widow of a Traitor

167 *Chiswick* Warwick Draper. pp 21, 29, 68, 78

168 *Moreana. VI.* 1965. 9–20

169 Roper. p xli. Moreana. No 4 & 5. (69–75)

170 Ibid

171 Roper v Royden. Dispositions in Chancery. (24/52)

172 Roper. p xli

173 *Letters and Papers. Henry VIII.* Vol XVI. No 744

174 *Feet of Fines.* Hertfordshire. P.R.O. Hilary. 28 Henry VIII

175 P.R.O. Tellers Rolls. E.405/110–116

176 *Letters and Papers. Henry VIII.* April 23, 1540. According to A.E. Reed this letter is still in the British Museum. *Times Literary Supplement* XXIX, 1970. p298

177 *Letters and Papers. Henry VIII.* 18 i. No evidence has been found so far of a pardon for John Elrington. A search in the Secret bag in the P.R.O. has proved negative, there is a conveyance of 29 acres of land by John Elrington, to the King, in 1542. (Survey of

London XXVII. Hackney Brooke House. pp59, 61n). Conveyance in Earl of Warwick's Records. Warwick 6625

178 *Letters and Papers. Henry VIII*. No 1166(38)

179 *Chelsea* Faulkner. p295

180 *Chelsea* Faulkner. p48

181 P.R.O. Bag of Secrets. Parcel XIII, Bundle I, for 1541. Recorded that John More sat on the jury at trial of Thomas Culpepper and Francis Dereham, both of whom were convicted of treasonable adultery with the King's wife, Catherine Howard.

182 Roper. p169 (note). Moreana XII. 47–48. p10

183 Hatfield Manor Court Rolls, 12/6 Hatfield Manor Papers, 2556

A Dainty Race of Children

184 Will of Thomas Elrington. P.C.C. 16 Bodfelde

185 Will of Sir Richard Harpur P.C.C. 15 Doggett

186 Manning and Bray. *History of Surrey*. 1810. p522–3

187 Faulkner. p70

188 *Moreana*. 1979. 63. Tome 2

189 Elrington Pedigree. *Excerpta Cantiana*. Thomas Streatfield

190 Ibid. Note 177

191 *Cambridge Antiquarian Society*. Vol XLI. p35

192 *Proceedings of Suffolk Institute of Archeology*. Vol IV. 1868. p111

193 Letter from Roger Asham to Lady Clarke. Jan 15, 1554. *Moreana* 1964. p80

194 Will of Sir Giles Alington. P.C.C. Windsor f 49

195 *The East Anglian*. Vol 10, 1903. Vision of Richard Alington. J.J. Muskett Notes and Queries. Series VII. i. p367

196 Will of Richard Alington. P.C.C. 7/ Street

197 *History of Long Melford*. William Parker. 1873. p329–330

198 James Howell. Letter to Dan Caldwell. May 20. 1619. Epistolae Ho-elianae

199 *The Shorter Strachey* Lady Hester Stanhope. O.U.P. 1980. p203

Epilogue

200 Works 1557, 1205

201 Dialogue of Comfort

202 Ro. Ba. p137

Bibliography

Basset, Bernard, S.J. *Born for Friendship*, Burns and Oates, 1965.

Beaver, A., *Memorials of old Chelsea*, 1892

Blakiston, H.E.D., *Trinity College, Oxford*, 1898

Brewer, J.S., ed., *Letters and Papers, Foreign and Domestic, Henry VIII*

Bridgett, T.E., *The Life of Blessed Thomas More*, 1891

Burke's Landed Gentry, 1938

Burke's Peerage, 1964

Calendar of Close Rolls, 1500

Chambers, R.W. *Thomas More*, Jonathan Cape 1935

Chapman, A.W., and Godfrey, W.H. *Some Famous Buildings and their story*, 1913

Chapman, Geoffrey, *Conscience Decides*, 1971

Colt, G.F.R., *History of Colt Family*, 1887

Copinger, *Manors of Suffolk*, 1905

Coussins, J.E., *History of Hertfordshire*, 1874

Davies, Randall, *Chelsea Old Church*

Davies, Randall, *The Greate House at Chelsea*, 1914

Draper, Warwick, *Chiswick*, 1923

Drummond, H., *History of Noble Families*, London 1846

Dugdale, William, *Antiquities of Warwickshire*, 1656

Dukes, *Antiquities of Shropshire*, 1844

Earwaker, J.P., *East Cheshire, Past and Present*, 1877

E.E.T.S., *More's Apologie*, 1930

East Anglian, The., Vol. 10, 1902

Edmunds, Jonathan, *A History of Latton*, 1980

Ellis, Henry, *History and Antiquities of Shoreditch*, 1798

Essex, Archaeological Society of, *New Series, Vol. VII*

Essex, Feet of Fines

Faulkner, Thomas, *History of Chelsea*, 1810

French, G.F., *Shakespearana Geneaologica*, 1869

Gough, Richard, *Sepulchral Monuments*, Vol. II

Harleian Society, *Visitation of Essex*, 1634

Hardwick and Tusmore, *History of Cottisford*, 1887

Harpsfield, *Appendix to, The Paris Newsletter* E.E.T.S. 1932

Harpsfield, Nicholas (Hitchcock E.V. ed.), *The Life and Death of Sir Thomas More* EETS, 1932

Hatfield and its People, W.E.A. books 2 & 6, 1960–61

Henry VIII, State Papers Vol. 1, 1830

Hertfordshire County Hall, *Public records*

Hine, Reginald L., *History of Hitchin*, 1928

Howards Letters, 1753

Home and Counties Magazine, IV, 1902

Kingdon, J.A., *Richard Grafton, Citizen and Grocer of London*, 1901

Library, The, Vol. VI, No. 4 1926

Macaulay, *History of England*, 1889

Marc'hadour, Germain, ed., *Moreana*, 1962–1980

McConica, James, *Thomas More*, 1977

Morant, Philip, *History and Antiquities of the County of Essex*, 1760–8

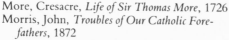

More, Cresacre, *Life of Sir Thomas More*, 1726

Morris, John, *Troubles of Our Catholic Fore-fathers*, 1872

Morrison, Stanley, *The Likeness of St. Thomas More*, Burns & Oates, 1963

Mynors, Roger, Translation by, *Letters of Erasmus*, Toronto University Edition of Erasmus' Letters

National Biography, Dictionary of, Oxford University Press

Newcourt, Richard, *Repetorium*, 1708

Notes and Queries, Series 7. Vol. I

Owen and Blakenor, *History of Shrewsbury, Vol. II*, 1825

Parker, Sir William, *History of Long Melford*, 1893

Parsons, Catherine E., *Horseheath Hall and its Owners, Proceedings of the Cambridge Antiquarian Society, Vol. XLI*, 1948

Pevsner, Nikolaus, *Essex*, 1979

Reed, A.W., *John Clements and His Books, The Library Vol. VI, No. 4*, 1926

Reynolds, E.E., *The Field is Won*, Burns and Oates, 1968

Reynolds, E.E., *Margaret Roper*, Burns and Oates, 1960

Reynolds, E.E., *The Trial of Sir Thomas More*, Burns and Oates, 1964

Ro. Ba., *The Life of Sir Thomas More*, E.E.T.S., 1950

Robinson, *History and Antiquities of Hackney*, 1842–1843

Rogers, E.F., ed. *Correspondence of Sir Thomas More*, Princetown University, 1947

Roper, William, ed. E.V. Hitchcock, *Life of Sir Thomas More Knight*, E.E.T.S., 1935

Routh, E.M., *St. Thomas More and His Friends*, Oxford University Press, 1934

Shanahan, D., *The Essex Recusant*, 1978

Staffordshire, Historical Collection of, 1939

Stapleton, Thomas, Trans. by Hallett, *Life of Thomas More*, 1928

Victoria County History for Cambs. and the Isle of Ely, Vol VI

Warnicke, Retha, *The Making of a Shrew, Rendezvous XV*, Arizona State University, 1980

Watney, J. *St. Thomas of Acon*, 1892

Weever, John, *Monumenta Antiqua*, 1767

Whibley, ed., *Halls Chronicle*

Whitaker, T.D., *History and Antiquities of the Deanery of Craven*, 1878

Williams, A. Garnons, *Formation and Development of a Yorkshire Estate, Stockeld Park*, 1978

Index

Aegidus, Petrus; (Peter Gillis): More's letter to, 31; Erasmus letter to, 32.

Aleyn, Joan: 103.

Alington, Alice: (see Alice Middleton).

Alington Chapel: (Elrington Chapel), Willesden, 53.

Alington, Cordell: daughter of Sir Richard Alington, married Sir John Stanhope, 133.

Alington, Cyril Argentine: Head Master of Eton, Dean of Durham, 50.

Alington, Sir Giles: Middleton of Stockeld Arms on Alington tombs at Horseheath Church, Cambs, 25; defence of Thomas Elrington, ward of Sir Thomas Lovell and son-in-law of Lady Alice, 36; succeeded to father's estate (1522); Sir John More his trustee while a minor; married first Ursula Drury, died (1522), one son, Robert; married secondly Alice Elrington, elder daughter of Lady Alice, 50; M.P. for Cambridge, 69; managed More's legal affairs; Cupbearer to King, 77; officiates at Anne Boleyn's Coronation, 78; draws up Bill of Complaint against John Lane for Lady Alice, 110; settles case against John Lane for Lady Alice, 112; brings writ against William Roper for compensation for loss of lands at Battersea, 112; co-defendant in sale of land in Hitchin, Ippollitts and Offley with his wife and Lady Alice, 114; assists Lady Alice in legal affairs, 117; will; copper ball from Siege of Boulogne, 126; buried with wife, Lady Alice's daughter, 128; made Sir William

Cordell one of his executors; outlived him; death (1586), 129.

Alington, Sir Giles: great grandson of Lady Alice; son-in-law of Sir Giles (senior); married Margaret Spencer, 125.

Alington, Sir Richard: second son of Sir Giles and Lady Alice Alington; age at More's death, 90; member of Lincoln's Inn, 118, childhood visions at Horseheath after More's death, 126; marries Jane Cordell, sister of Sir William Cordell, Master of the Rolls, 127; three daughters, two survived, Cordell and Mary; conflict over New Religion; illness; death (1561); bequest for lively remembrance of Passion; tomb in P.R.O. Museum, Chancery Lane, 128; Bishop Allen and Father Richard Bristow write of his visions, 129.

Alington, William: married Elizabeth, daughter of Sir John Argentine; brought office of Cupbearer to King into Alington family, 50.

Allen, Dr William: (see Sir Richard Alington).

Ammonio, Andrea: Latin Secretary to Henry VIII; teasing remarks on Lady Alice's nose, 9, 5, 56; outstays welcome at More household, 31; Erasmus' letter to, 34.

Apologie of St Thomas More, 77.

Aragon, Queen Catherine: friendship with More; More's discussion of divorce, 66.

Arderns of Cottisford, Oxfordshire, 12.

Alice, daughter of William Ardern, 12.

John, son of William Ardern, 12.

family portrait, 17; sent to Erasmus, 58.

Basing, Hants: Home of 5th Marquis of Winchester, husband of Lady Alice's great great great grand-daughter, Jane Savage; beseiged in Civil War, 130.

Bassett, Father Bernard: *Born for Friendship*, description of Lady Alice, 6; his reasons for More marrying Alice, 31.

Baynards, Surrey: property of Bray family; Mary, Lady Alice's granddaughter lived here on marriage to Sir Edward Bray, the younger, 123; Elizabeth, daughter of Roper, 2nd wife of Sir Edward lived here; kept More's head under stairs; son Reynold born (1555); sold to Sir George More of Loosley, kinsman of Sir John More's 3rd wife; drive admired by John Evelyn, 124.

Beaver's Memorials of Old Chelsea: More epitaph and Arms in Chelsea Church, 19.

Bekynsale, John: involved in Plot of Prebendaries of Canterbury, 115.

Blunt, Reginald: account in *Times* of removal of More coffins to St Luke's, Chelsea, 118.

Bohun, Humphrey: father of Sir John; home at Midhurst, Sussex, 15 (see Anne Ardern).

Bohun, Sir John: 15; dies (1501), *22* (see Anne Ardern).

Bohun, Katherine: wife of Sir Peter Ardern of Markhall, Essex, 11, 15.

Bohun, Mary: (see Mary Ardern), 15, 63.

Bohun, Ursula: see Ursula Ardern, 15; married Robert Southwell, 15, 63.

Boleyn, Queen Anne: More's dismay at King's infatuation with, 66; her jealousy and dislike of More, 68; Coronation, 78; persistence that More should swear to complete Act of Supremacy, 81; demands that refusal to swear be made treason, 86–87, executed (1536), 92,

Bolt, Robert: *A Man for All Seasons*; description of Lady Alice, 10.

Bonvisi, Antonio: silk merchant from Lucca; great friend of Mores; bought lease of Crosby Hall from More; description of; More and Lady Alice at supper party, 52–53; gives More camulet

robe, 107; fled to Louvain, 116.

Bouge, Father John: letter to Catherine Manne on More's hasty marriage, 4.

Boulogne, Siege of: Sir Giles Alington brings home large copper gilt ball now in Naseby Church, Northants, 126.

Boxhall, John: Warden of Winchester, 127.

Bray family: Lords of Manor of Chelsea, Eaton Bray, Shere Vachery, 117.

Bray, Beatrix: sister of Sir Edward Bray, junior; married Thomas Elrington, grandson of Lady Alice, 124, 117.

Bray, Lord Edmund: inherits estates of Sir Reginald Bray; account of funeral, 123.

Bray, Sir Edward, the elder: of Baynards; bought Shere Vachery from elder brother, Lord Edmund; inherited Eaton Bray on Lord Edmund's death, 123.

Bray, Sir Edward, the younger: married 1st, Mary Elrington, Lady Alice's grand-daughter; accompanies funeral of Lord John, 124; marries 2nd Elizabeth, More's Roper grand-daughter, 115; inherited Eaton Bray (1558), 124.

Bray, Elizabeth: daughter of William and Margaret Roper; given More's head on mother's death, 115; 2nd wife of Sir Edward Bray; died (1560), 115, 124; lived at Baynards, 124.

Bray, Sir Reginald: executor to will of Sir Richard Harpur, 21; Lady Alice's granddaughter, Mary Elrington, marries his great nephew; associate of Sir Richard Harpur; Knight of Garter, architect of St George's Chapel, Windsor, and Henry VII Chapel, Westminster Abbey; Lord of Manor of Chelsea, Shere Vachery, Eaton Bray; died (1503); no children; estates left to Lord Edmund Bray, 122, 123.

Bray, Reynold, the first: only son of Sir Edward Bray and Mary Elrington; pre-deceased his father (1577), 124.

Bray, Reynold, the second; half brother to Reynold Bray the first; son of Sir Edward Bray and Elizabeth, daughter of Margaret and William Roper; born 1555; owing to death of elder half-brother,

(1511); neighbour of Lady Alice in Essex, 21; early days of marriage to More, 30; body removed to Chelsea, 56.

Colt, John: of Netherhall, Essex; father of Jane, 1st wife of More, 13, 14.

Colt, Magdalen: née Middleton, 12.

Colt, Thomas: grandfather of Jane, 1st wife of More, 21 (see Edward IV).

Colt, Thomas: younger brother of Jane, 1st wife of More, 12, 13.

Conyers, Lady: kinswoman of Cuthbert Tunstall; picture of More for Elizabeth Dauncey, 103.

Cordell, Jane: sister of Sir William Cordell, Master of Rolls; marries Lady Alice's grandson, Sir Richard Alington, 127.

Cordell, Sir William; Master of Rolls; acquired Long Melford Hall, Suffolk, 129 (see Jane Cordell).

Corsham Court: portrait of Lady Alice, now in Switzerland, 58.

Cottisford: (see Arderns of).

Cranevelt, Francis: More's letter about wives, 31.

Cranmer, Thomas: Archbishop of Canterbury; letter to Cromwell, 81; supresses Plot of Prebendaries of Canterbury, 115.

Cresacre, Anne: joined More household as More's ward when 3 years old; Lady Alice knew family; born (1511); Holbein's drawing, 34, 35; married John More (1529), 35–36, 54, 69; joins school, 41; love of jewellery, 43; laughs at More's hair shirt, 44; family portrait, 58; inherits Barnborough on marriage, 69; farewell to More, 102; John More dependant on her fortune; returned to Barnborough (1559); marries George West, 116; daughter by John More marries George West's son, John; their descendants married into Sackville family; founded Sackville-West family; died (1577); buried at St Peter's, Barnborough, 116.

Cresacre, Edward: of Barnborough, Yorkshire; father of Anne Cresacre, 34.

Creyke, Agnes: mother of John Middleton; brother Thomas married Jane Ardern

daughter of Thomas Ardern of Marton, Yorks, 24 (see Middleton Pedigree).

Cromwell, Sir Richard: nephew of Thomas Cromwell; great grandfather of Sir Oliver Cromwell; accompanies More to Tower, 81.

Cromwell, Thomas: leads attack on More, 77; letter from Cranmer, 81; letter from Lady Alice, 93; ruined by Richard Rich, 100; Giles Heron's sons plead for father's life, 114.

Crosby Hall: leased by More in (1523); lease sold to Bonvisi, 52; Hall moved to Chelsea (1910), 53.

Dacre, Lady: leaves Great House, Chelsea to Lord Burghley, 59.

Dauncey, William: marriage to Elizabeth More (1525), 53; estates in Hertfordshire, Buckinghamshire, 53; M.P. for Thetford, Norfolk; involved in Plot of Prebendaries of Canterbury, pardoned, 115; inherited property from father in (1545), 118.

Denecourt, Kent: Elrington Manor; left to Lady Alice's daughter, Alice Elrington for life, 38, 93, 124.

Dialogue of Heresies: St Thomas More, 78.

Divorce: King's Great Matter, 66, 69; More avoids giving opinion, 69; More refuses to sign appeal to Pope, 71; More submits Henry's case to Parliament (1531), 71.

Doddington (Ducklington), Oxfordshire: property of More, 73; given to Sir Henry Norris, 92.

Downes Farm: 70, 73 (see Hatfield).

Drew, Richard: Fellow of All Souls, Oxford; Tutor to More's School, 42.

Drury, Ursula: 1st wife of Sir Giles Alington; one son, Robert; died (1522), 50.

Duchy of Lancaster; 15 (see Sir Peter Ardern); Enfield.

Dymoke, Sir Andrew: 3rd husband of Elizabeth Ardern (see Elizabeth Ardern); mentioned in deed with Sir Richard Harpur (1486), (1489); Baron of Exchequer (1500); died (1508), 22.

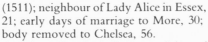

Edward IV: Thomas Colt his Chancellor of Exchequer, 21.

Elizabeth II, Queen: direct Descendant of Lady Alice More, 136.

Elizabeth of Glamis, The Queen Mother: direct descendant of Lady Alice More; youngest daughter of Claude, 14th Earl of Strathmore; born St. Paul's Walden, Hertfordshire, (1900); married Duke of York, (1923); Queen Consort (1937); daughter Queen Elizabeth II, 134, 135.

Eltham Ordinance: (1526), 66.

Elrington, Alice: (see Alice Middleton).

Elrington, Edward: son of Thomas and Beatrix Elrington, great grandson of Lady Alice; married Margaret, daughter of Sir John Spencer of Althorpe, Northants, 125.

Elrington, John: younger son of Thomas and Alice Elrington, grandson of Lady Alice; born 1522; second cousin to More's children, 40–41; one year old when father died, 50; twelve years old when More's letter from Tower reached Horseheath; branded as filthy traitor, 90; arrested and condemned for part in Plot of Prebendaries of Canterbury, 115; moved to Horseheath Hall, 122.

Elrington, Mary: daughter of Thomas and Alice Elrington; granddaughter of Lady Alice; born (1520); second cousin to More's children, 40–41; three years old when father died, 50; married Sir Edward Bray, junior, 123, 117; moved to Horseheath Hall, 122; lived at Baynards, Surrey; one son, 123, 124; (see Reynold Bray, the first).

Elrington, Mary: daughter of Thomas Elrington, junior; maried Lord Morley, who bought Markhall from Thomas Shaa, 125, 22.

Elrington, Thomas senior: grand-son of Sir John Elrington, Treasurer of household to Edward IV; son of Simon Elrington: Ward of Sir Thomas Lovell, 36, 48; married Alice Middleton, eldest daughter of Lady Alice More, 38, 48; More his executor, 50; Lovell makes restitution to his estate in will, 36; his property, 38;

Erasmus' description of him, 40; three children, 40–41; second cousin to More's children, 41; devotion to More's son John; died (1523), 50, 144; wished to be buried at Hoggeston (Hoxton); buried in Elrington Chantry, St Leonard's Church, Shoreditch, 48; mentioned with affection by More in last letter from Tower; had post in Treasury as Teller, 48; Alice his executor with More, 50; son Thomas married Beatrix Bray, 124, 117.

Elrington, Thomas junior: elder son of Thomas and Alice Elrington; born (1521); second cousin to More's children, 40–41, 48, 124; two years old when father died, 50, 124; thirteen years old when More's letter from Tower reached Horseheath, 90; devotion to More's grandson Thomas More; left him Manor at Willesden, 125; moved to Horseheath Hall, 122; inherited Denecourt, Brenzett, Kent, Willesden Manor, Fosham Manor, Yorkshire; married Beatrix Bray, 124; son Edward married Margaret, daughter of Sir John Spencer of Althorpe, Northants, 125.

Elyot, Sir Thomas: married Margaret à Barrow; pupils at More's school, 41.

Enfield Chase: lease held by Sir Peter Ardern; see Duchy of Lancaster; lease left to Elizabeth Ardern; Ardern association with Tudors; Richard III transferred lease to Duke of Buckingham; More and George Colt purchase land near Enfield, 23.

Epping, Essex: home of Harpur family, 15

Erasmus, Desiderius: description of Lady Alice and More family, 38; drawing of family portrait sent to him, 17, 58; describes John More, 29; admires likeness in family sketch, 31, 58; outstays welcome in More household, 31; letter to Peter Gilles, 32; stays at St Thomas of Acon; described by E.M. Routh as difficult guest, 34; admits Lady Alice apt musical pupil, 37; said first six years of marriage to Lady Alice happiest in More's life, 37; letter to Budé on Lady

expense; lived in household as tutor and physician, 42.

Ippolletts, Herts; lands held by Lady Alice; sold (1536), 114.

Ireland, John: Roper's chaplain at Well Hall Kent; involved in plot of prebendaries of Canterbury; condemned to death, 115, 125.

Ireland, Roger: (see John Ireland).

Johnson, Ben: poem to Jane Savage, 5th Marchioness of Winchester, 130, 132.

Kellvedon, Essex: (see Filiols (Felix Hall)).

Kemp, Marjorie: daughter of William Kemp of Spains Hall, Finchingfield, Essex; niece by marriage to More, married George Cavendish; neighbour of Arderns, 68.

Kingston, Sir William: Constable of Tower; accompanies More to Tower after trial; describes scene to Roper, 102, 106.

King's Great Matter: see divorce; More takes a stand on, 77.

Kratzer, Nicholas: tutor to More's children, 17, 42.

Lane, John: speculator in property; litigation with Lady Alice over Sutton Court, Chiswick; Bill of complaint against him, 110, 112.

Lambeth Palace: More summoned to take Oath, refuses Oath, 80, (see St Thomas More).

Larke, John: rector of Chelsea; involved in Plot of Prebendaries of Canterbury; condemned to death (1544), 115; Lady Alice given lease of his house, (see Faulkner, Thomas).

Latton, Essex: Church of St Mary-at-Latton, 11, 14, 18; Manors of Latton and Markhall, 15, 16; Chantry Chapel of Arderns, 15; Sir Richard Harpur leaves manor to wife Elizabeth, (see Harpur).

Lawrence, Sir John: More epitaph re-built by; redesigned by (1644), 18; confusion

in Ardern Arms, 18, 19.

Lincoln's Inn: 75, 118, 127.

Louvain: (see Clements, Bonvisi).

London: (see Tower of); Churches - St Stephens, Walbrook, 4; St Katherine Coleman, 25, 127; St Leonard's Shoreditch, 48; St Paul's, 33, 80; St Peter ad Vincular, 108; St Luke's, Chelsea, 119; Henry VII's chapel, Westminster Abbey, 123.

Long Melford Hall, Suffolk: acquired by Sir William Cordell (1547), 129; left house to sister, Jane Alington, (1582); Lady Alice's great grand-daughter, Mary Savage inherits from Jane; passed down to 1st Viscount Rocksavage; household there of Lady Alice's descendants admired by James Howell, 129–30.

Lovell, Sir Thomas: Survey or Court of Wards; guardian of Thomas Elrington; deprived him of some property; died (1524); made restitution to Elrington estate in will, 36, 48.

Lyndsay House: in Cheyne Walk, Chelsea; site of More's original farm, 76, 77.

Macaulay, Thomas: 108

Maclagan, Michael, Richmond Herald: 10.

Manne, Dame Catherine: letter from Father Bouge, (see Bouge).

Mattock, Nicholas: beneficiary under will of Sir John Shaa, 22; co-executor with Lady Alice of John Middleton's will; owned property in Hitchin, 23.

Markhall, Essex: home of Arderns, 14; bought by Sir Peter Ardern (1446), 15; left estate to wife for life, then daughter Anne Bohun, 15; adjacent to Latton, 16; Lady Alice heraldic heiress of Markhall Arderns, 17; younger branch of Arderns, 18; sold by Anne Bohun to Sir John Shaa, 22; estate passes to Sir John Shaa's son Edmund (1503), 22; due to Edmund's insanity, More custodian of property including Markhall, 22, 97; on death of Edmund, sold to Henry Parker, Lord Morley, 22.

Maynard, Theodore: description of Lady Alice, 6.

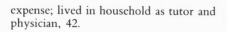

from King and Queen, 69; spends more time at Chelsea, 69; member of Fraternity of Christ's Church Canterbury (1530); describes father; comes into father's property, Downs Farm & Waltrapps, Herts, 70; refuses to sign appeal to Pope on divorce; receives clergy's final submission; resigns Lord Chancellorship; Lady Alice's influence on his rise to power, and fall, 71; declining health, 72; income before retirement; income after retirement; estates after retirement, 73; suggests children pay their keep when at Chelsea, 75; Confutation of Tyndale's answer (1532); letter to John Frith; Apologie; attacked by Thomas Cromwell; offered £50,000 by Bishops, 77; refers to financial position; mention of Lady Alice's wealth; Dialogue of Heresies; refuses to go to Coronation, 78; warned of danger by Norfolk; fear of having to take Oath on Act of Succession; tries too late to settle his affairs, 79; goes with Roper to St Paul's; receives summons while at Barge to go to Lambeth, 80; Roper's description of; last morning at Chelsea; goes to Lambeth; refuses to take oath; stays with Abbot of Westminster; committed to Tower; letter from Cranmer to Cromwell; refuses to send gold chain back to Lady Alice, 80–81; 1st letter from Tower to Margaret Roper; visits from Lady Alice, 82; cell open during day, 84; sorrow at letter from Margaret Roper, 85; his reply; worry about safety of family, 85, 86; fear of physical suffering; Alice Alington's letter, 87; joint reply by Margaret and More; affection for Alice Alington, 88–90; Act of Attainder against; conditions in Tower changed; money owing to King; poverty deliberately exaggerated; increasing illness, 91, 92; deprived of manors of Ducklington, Fringford, Barley Park, South, 92; warns Margaret Roper of house searches, 92–93; misses Lady Alice and family; suggestion of family quarrels, 94; poem

to Henry VIII, 96; Act of Attainder; four interrogations; visit of Richard Rich, 97; Rich accompanied by Southwell, kinsman of Lady Alice, to collect books, 98; account of Rich's character at trial, 98, 100; reminds Audeley of his right to address Court; addresses Court, 101; (see Paris News Letter); condemned to hang, drawing and quartering; says farewell to children; visit by Lady Alice before execution, 102; last letter to Margaret Roper unfinished, 103; Sir Thomas Pope informs him of time of execution; death changed to beheading, 104, 106; Lady Alice outlives him by 17 years, 117; final burial place; extract from *Times* on final burial place of More family, 119; descendants of, 120.

More, Thomas, jnr: son of John More and Anne Cresacre; left Willesden Manor by Thomas Elrington, jnr, 125.

Moreton, John: wealthy landowner; went insane; ward of More, 36.

Morley, Lord: bought Markhall estate from Thomas Shaa, 22; married Lady Alice's granddaughter, Mary Elrington, 125.

National Portrait Gallery: copy of Holbein family group much altered, 59; 'King's Good Servant' Exhibition, 71.

Netherhall, Essex: home of Colt family, 13, 14, 19; (see Colt family). More returns there with Jane to sort out matrimonial differences, 30.

New College, Oxford: Harpsfield Fellow of, 6.

Newcourt, Richard: *Repertorium*; More epitaph, (see Chelsea Old Church).

Norfolk, Duke of: More speaks of declining health, 72; warns More of danger in refusing coronation invitation, 79; interrupts More's speech at trial, 102.

Norris, Sir Henry: acquires More's manors of Ducklington, Fringford Barley Park (1535), 92; favourite of Anne Boleyn; executed (1536), 92.

Northampton: Bohun's Earls of, 15.

Northumberland, Duke of: ruined by Richard Rich, 100.

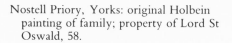

More's trial, 98.

Spencer, Sir John of Althorpe: daughter Margaret marries Edward Elrington, great grand-son of Lady Alice; direct ancester of Princess of Wales, 147.

Spencer, Margaret: (see Sir John Spencer); left all her property to Elrington family, 125.

Stanford Rivers, Essex: property of Sir John Skreene, 15.

Stanhope, Lady Hester: daughter of 3rd Earl Stanhope; born (1776), 9, 133; characteristics in common with Lady Alice, 134; (see William Pitt).

Stanhope, Sir John: married Cordell, daughter of Sir Richard Alington, 133.

Stanhope, Philip, 1st Earl Chesterfield: Lady Alice's great great grandson; born (1584); eleven sons by first wife Catherine; Bretby sacked; son Philip killed at Shelford; eldest son John died (1625); second son Henry died (1634); 4th son Ferdinand killed (1644); epitaph by Aston Cokayne; 2nd marriage to Anne, widow of Sir Humphrey Ferras; one son Alexander; Lady Hester Stanhope descended from 2nd marriage, 133.

Stanhope, Philip, 2nd Earl of Chesterfield; married 1st, Ann Percy, daughter of Earl of Northumberland, no children; 2nd marriage Lady Elizabeth Butler; daughter Elizabeth married John Lyon, 4th Earl of Strathmore, 133, 134.

Stanhope, Philip Dormer, 4th Earl of Chesterfield: direct descendant of Lady Alice; letters to son, 134.

Stanhope, Philip Henry, 5th Earl of Chesterfield; Founder of National Portrait Gallery; More Exhibition, 134.

Stapleton, Thomas: *Life of More*; opinion of Lady Alice, 6; preserved More's letter to Gunnell, 42.

Staverton, Frances: daughter of More's sister Jane; joins More school, 41.

Stockeld Park, Yorkshire: home of Middletons; Arms of Stockeld Middletons, 23, 25.

Stokehide (Stockhide) Herts: property

owned by More, Alice collects rents up to her death, 118.

Strachey, Lytton: description of Lady Hester Stanhope's nose, 9.

Strathmore, John Lyon, 4th Earl of Strathmore: (see Philip Stanhope), 2nd Earl of Chesterfield, 134.

Strathmore, John, 5th Earl of Strathmore: first direct descendant of Lady Alice to bear Strathmore title; killed at Sherriffmuir (1715), 134.

Strathmore, Claude, 14th Earl: direct descendant of Lady Alice; father of Queen Mother, 134.

Succession, Act of, (1534): 80.

Supremacy, the King's: More receives final submission of clergy (1532), 71; Lady Alice's attitude to, 71; refusal to take Oath changed from misprision of treason to treason, 86–7.

Sutton Court, Chiswick: property of Mores; litigation between Lady Alice and John Lane; description of; owned by Oliver Cromwell's daughter, Countess of Falconberg, 110–112.

Symands, J.: plans of Great House at Chelsea before alterations; in archives at Hatfield House, 59.

Thorne, Thomas: of Northamptonshire; married Alice Ardern of Cottisford; (see Arderns of Cottisford).

Thorpe, John: plans of suggested alterations for Great House, Chelsea for Lord Burghley, 59.

Tower of London: Governor's house in, 2; More's son John imprisoned in, 29; More taken to, 81; at time of More's imprisonment, 82; Zoo, 84; More's return to after trial, 102; Royal Mint in, 104; St Peter ad Vincula, 108.

Trinity College, Oxford: (see Thomas Pope), Founder.

Tudor, Owen: grandfather of Henry VII; natural father of Sir David Owen, husband of Mary Bohun, cousin of Lady Alice; granddaughter of Sir Peter Ardern, 15.

Acknowledgements

I would like to acknowledge with grateful thanks, the help and encouragement the following people have given me in bringing this book out of the 'shadows':

Barbara Bates, Archivist, Lincoln's Inn; William Bell, Cottisford House, Oxon; Mrs Handa Bray, Shere, Surrey; The Rev. R Bryden, former Vicar of Eastrington, Yorkshire; Mrs Betty Case of Saffron Walden, Essex; The Lord Cholmondeley; The Rev. L.E.M. Claxton, Rector of St Olave's, Hart Street and St Katherine Coleman; Mrs Mary Dawson, Horseheath Park Farm, Cambs; The Rev. H.R. Davis, Vicar of Eaton Bray, Beds; Mr R. Dawes, Divisional Librarian, Kent County Library; Mrs Hever. A. Collier, Looseley House, Guildford; Mr Stephen Donnelly; Mr Christopher Elrington, Editor, Victoria County History; Mr M.W. Farr, County Archivist, Warwick County Council; Mr Charles Goldie of Myddeleton House, Saffron Walden, Essex; Mrs R Gough, Stockeld Park, Yorkshire; Mr Victor Gray, County Archivist, Essex; Mr Peter Gwyn; Miss Marion Halford, County Archivist, Shropshire; Professor Hubert Herbrugen, Düsseldorf University; Mr John Rowland Hunt, Boreatton, Salop; Mr Michael Maclagan, Richmond Herald; The Hon. Mary Marten, Crichel, Dorset; The Lord Methuen, Corsham Court, Wilts; Lady Morse; Sir Roger and Lady Mynors; Sir Richard Hyde-Parker, Melford Hall, Long Melford; The Rev. John Pratt, Vicar of St Mary-at-Latton, Essex; The Late Mrs Mary H.V. Probert; Lieut. Col. Richard Probert; Mrs D. Randall, Assistant Archivist, Staffordshire County Council; Dr R. Robson, Trinity College, Cambs; The Rev. Peter Ronayne, Vicar of St Leonard's Shoreditch; Mr John Rowlands, Deputy Keeper, British Museum; Mr David Starkey, London University; Dr David Smith, Borthwick Institute, York; D.A.J. Taylor, Archivist, The Grocers Company; The Rev. Leighton Thomson, Rector of Chelsea Old Church; Mr S. Tongue, Archivist, Rose Lypton Library, Hackney; The Rev. Chad Varah, Rector of St Stephen's, Walbrook; Miss Rachael Warren, Shere, Surrey; Mgr. James Wilder, Church of St Thomas More, New York; Mr R.H. Harcourt Williams, Archivist, Hatfield House.

Especially, thanks go to my late husband, Sir Arthur (Thomas) Norrington, because without his constant encouragement, I would have been tempted to give up the search for Lady Alice long ago.

List of Subscribers

Diana J. Adams
Joyce Doreen Adams
Agnes Albert
The Reverend Hugh Oliver Albin
The Rector, Allen Hall, Chelsea
Hazel M. Allport
Ambrose Swasey Library, New York
Ambrosia Books Ltd.
Ampleforth Abbey Library
Appleby, Myers & Clarke
Robert and Serena Armstrong
David Ashworth
Mrs E.M. Atkin
Eleanor Aylen

Bill Bailey
Frank Ballin
Jean E. Ballantyne
Sir David Barran
Miss Anne E. Barker
Reverend Bernard Basset
Anna Battista
John Bayliss
Countess Beatty
Dr. William Beautyman
Michael J. Bellis
Miss M. Belcher
Mrs E. Benians
Mrs Spencer Bernard
Dr. Maria Lisa Bertagnoni
Josephine Birchenough
Sir Basil Blackwell
B.H. Blackwell Ltd.
Gerald Bonner, University of Durham
Helen Boyd
Alison and Tony Brabbin
Brown, Picton and Hornby Libraries

Reverend C.B. Brown
Bryn Mawr College Library, U.S.A.
Peter Bucknill
Mr & Mrs Hugh Buchanan
Dr. Roberta Buchanan
Köselsche Buchhandlung
John and Shirley Bush
Mrs C.D.N. Butler
Arthur V. Butler
Audrey M. Butler
Mrs Moira Buxton

Campion Hall
Philip Caraman
Sarah Carolan
Mrs W.E. Carslake
Mrs Rose Caunt
R.T.S. Charlton
Marie–Françoise Christensen
Churchill College Library
Poor Clares, Woodchester, Gloucester
Anthony John Sheil Clarke
Marion Clark
Mrs Robert Collier
Congregation of Jesus and Mary
Graham Cooper
Community of the Sisters of the Church
Sister Irene Cornelius
Judge F. Joseph Cornish
The County Archivist, Hertfordshire
  Record Office
Elizabeth Cramp
Reverend C.W. Crawford
Alexandra M. Cullum
Philip D. Cullum
Monsignor Thomas W. Cunningham

Sheila Davin
M. Genevieve Devereux
Lieut. Col. and Mrs John Dingwall
Lady Downe
Dressers (Stationers) Ltd.
William Duffy

Charles and Joan Erwood
Essex Record Office
Mary Edwina Evans
Lady Agnes Eyston
Mrs Eyston
Mrs Michael Charles Eyston
Thomas More Eyston

Miss Bridget E. Fann
Farm Street Library
H. Richmond Fisher
Professor and Mrs H.A. Fitzpatrick
James Joseph Fitzpatrick
Dame Bede Foord
Alistair Fox
Sir Frank and Lady Francis
Miss M. Frazer
Lady Fyffe

Mrs M.A. Gale
Charles Gallo
Eileen Garnham
The General Theological Seminary, New
   York
Albert J. Geritz
Mrs Ann Glossop
Charles Goldie
Charles Gordon
Mrs Philip Gorman
Damian Grace
Mrs J. Peter Grace
Sheila Graham
Mrs Graham Greene
Lavinia M. Greenwood
Mr & Mrs J. Griffiths
F.E. Christopher Grundy
Amadeu T. De Mesquita Guimaraes
Richard Thomas Guy
Selwyn Guy
Peter Gwyn

Barry J. Hagan
Ruthven and Zaida Hall
Ronald and Jay Hamilton
Hampshire County Library
H.L.H. Harrison
G.A. Harper
Lady Dorothy Hart
Dieter Hau
Agnes B. and James V. Hayes
J.M. Hayward
Hans and Mies Heilen, Claerhoudt
Professor Hubertus Schulte Herbrüggen,
   University of Düsseldorf
Hertfordshire Library Service
Professor & Mrs T.F. Hewer
Heythrop College
Arthur Edward Hinds
Gregory Thomas More Hinds
Mrs E. Howard

Institut interuniversitaire pour l'étude de la
   Renaissance et de l'Humanisme
   (Université Libre de Bruxelles)

The Holt Jackson Book Co. Ltd.
Jerome Dawson Memorial, New York
Harold B. Jewell
D.J. Johnston
Mrs I.G. Jones

Barbara Jean Kelly
Eileen Kent
John Keohane
Michael Keohane
Dr. Lee Cullen Khanna
William Aloysius Joachim Kinsella
Darrell Kok

P. Terrence Lamb
Jennifer Lane
Elizabeth Land
Mrs Rita T. Larner
D.S. Laughton
Kenneth Patrick Lefebvre, Q.C.
Rudolf Leinemann
Dr. & Mrs I. Lenox-Smith
F.J. Levitt
Mrs O.E. Lewinski
Piers Litherland

Elizabeth Littlejohn
Llanelli Public Library
Peggy Loader
London Library
Robert Lomax
The Countess of Longford
Mr Hugh Loughran
Mrs Patricia Loughran

Mrs G.P.S. MacPherson
Bishop Gerald Mahon
Mr & Mrs Sam Mainds
Madame Jocelyne Malhomme
Miss M. Mandville
Father G. Marc'hadour
The Hon. Mrs Marten
Judge Peter Mason, Q.C.
Miss Alison Mason
Mrs Anne Matthews
Mr B. Mawhinney
Mrs Cuthbert Mayne
James McConica
Reverend William G. McConalogue
Reverend Arthur McCormack
Dr. Elizabeth McCutcheon
Hugh P. McFadden
Nigel McGilchrist
McGill University Libraries, Quebec
Andrew M. McLean
Mrs Seymour Mead
Virginia Shaw Medlen
John Menzies Library Services Ltd.
Clarence H. Miller
Mr & Mrs A.W. Milliner
Mr & Mrs Donald J. Millus
Marjorie Mockler
Hans Moëll
Ruth Moir
Association Amici Thomae Mori
The Amici Thomae Mori of Great Britain
Sir Jeremy and Lady Morse
Francis and Geraldine Murray
Roger and Lavinia Mynors

The New York Public Library
The Newman–Mowbray Bookshop,
    Oxford
Canon Donald Nicholson
Humphrey and Frances Norrington

R.A.C. Norrington
William V. Nuetzel

M. Rosemary O'Brien
Mr & Mrs P.R. Odgers
Mrs Joyce W. Oliver
John O'Neill
Oscott College

Ann Parker
Anita Parker
Sir Richard Hyde Parker, Bart
Geoffrey de C. Parmiter
Sister Mary Barbara Pearce
Sally Peck
Frank J. Pegnam
Marianne Perkins-Contesse
George M. St. Peter
Arthur Petty
C.G. and C.M. Phillips
Dr. Margaret Mann Phillips
Professor R.S. Pilcher
Raymond Plant, Q.C.
Peter and Caroline Please
Mr C. Normand Poirier
Pontifical Institute of Mediaeval Studies,
    Toronto
A.K. Potter
Judith Prendergast
Ellen Preston
Priory of Our Lady of Good Counsel
Lieut. Col. R.H.C. Probert, O.B.E.
Doris M. Pullen

Lord and Lady Quinton

Elizabeth Ralph
Rt. Hon. Lord Rawlinson, Q.C.
Redbridge Public Library
Dr. May Reed
P.M. Birch Reynardson
Michael Richards
Miss Eileen Riches
Vivian and Anne Ridler
Marjorie A. Riley
Robin Risley
Brenda Rivett
Elizabeth G. Roberts
Mrs E.T. Robinson

Frances Robson
Mrs L.P. Roper
Miss E.M. Rose
John Rose
M.C. Rosenfield
The Royal Library, Windsor Castle
Reverend Richard R. Russell
J.L. Russell
George Ryan
Xavier Ryckmans
Stephen Ryle

Laura E. Salt
Angele Botros Samaan
Dr. Peter Sampo
Pippa Sandford
Mr J.C. Saunders
P.A. Sawada
Lord Saye
Reverend H. and Mrs Grant Scarfe
Robert Schneebeli, Zurich
Reverend Karl G. Schroeder
A.E. de Schryver
W. Hartley Seed — Booksellers
Howard A. Seitz
Colon C. Settle
E.H. Seward
Rosalind Shakespear
Nigel Shakespear
Joan Shaw
Lord Sherfield
Viscountess Sidmouth
Sisters of Jesus and Mary, Thame
Judy Sladden
Mrs L.W. Smallwood
David Baird-Smith
Mr & Mrs P.R. Smith
Reverend William J.T. Smith
David and Sally Smout
Albert and Constance Sprilyan
Society of St. John the Evangelist
Shirley Stacey
Mgr. Anthony Stark
Starkmann Library Services Ltd.
St. John Fisher College Library, Tasmania
St. John Seminary Library, Brighton,
    U.S.A.
St. John's University Law Library (More
    Collection), New York, U.S.A.

St. Joseph's Convent, Ontario
St. Joseph's School, Thame
St. Paul's College Library, Winnipeg
St. Thomas More Chapel, Yale University
Church of St. Thomas More, New York
Stevens & Brown Ltd.
Chauncey Stillman
Majie Padberg Sullivan
J.H.G. Sunnucks
Yoshinori Suzuki

C.W. Taylor
Mrs R. Glyn Thomas
Thomas More Prep/Marian High, Hays,
    Kansas
Sister M. Geraldine Thompson
C.E. Leighton Thomson
John Thomson
Robert Threlfall
Chris and Anita Tolley
Stuart and Douglas Tolley
Gerald Tomlinson
Joan Tomlinson
Mark Tomlinson
Rt. Reverend Mgr. G.A. Tomlinson
Dr. Noel J. Toups
Peter and Alex Tucker
Anne Mary Turner

University of San Francisco
University of North Carolina at Chapel
    Hill
University of Washington Libraries
Upholland Northern Institute
John Murdo Urquhart

David Vellacott
Venerable English College, Italy
Dr. G. Villa

Christine Walker
Dorothy R. Ward
Philip Warman
Louis B. Warren
Miss R. Warren
Mrs A. Waterlow
The Reverend Fr. Peter Maurice Waters

Colin Vincent Watson of Blagdon
Mary M. Webb
Mother Catherine Margaret Wells
Westminster Cathedral Bookshop
Franklin B. William Jr.
Dr. & Mrs J.R.B. Williams

Miss R. Williamson
Mrs Chester Wilmot
Sir Brian and Lady Windeyer
The Worshipful Company of Mercers
Sir Denis and Lady Wright

DATE DUE

APR 2 0 '89			

The 1979 State Opening of Parliament with some notable descendants
Lord Cholmondeley; The Lord Great Chamberlain; Michael Maclagan